北京生态社区

北京市海淀区南沙河区域"反规划"

Beijing Ecological Community

Negative Planning in Nanshahe, Haidian District, Beijing

俞孔坚　阿德里安·布莱克韦尔　斯蒂芬·欧文　等编著

Edited by Kongjian Yu, Adrian Blackwell, and Stephen Ervin

哈佛大学设计学院 景观建筑与城市规划与设计系研究报告　2014年春季

A Studio Research Report from the Harvard University Graduate School of Design
Departments of Landscape Architecture and Urban Planning and Design, Spring 2014

中国建筑工业出版社

图书在版编目（CIP）数据

北京生态社区　北京市海淀区南沙河区域"反规划" /
俞孔坚等编著.—北京：中国建筑工业出版社，2015.8
ISBN 978-7-112-18250-3

Ⅰ．①北…　Ⅱ．①俞…　Ⅲ．①社区建设－生态环境建
设－研究－北京市－汉、英　Ⅳ．①D669.3

中国版本图书馆CIP数据核字（2015）第149389号

责任编辑：郑淮兵　焦　阳
责任校对：姜小莲　刘梦然

北京生态社区

北京市海淀区南沙河区域"反规划"

俞孔坚　阿德里安·布莱克韦尔　斯蒂芬·欧文　等编著
*
中国建筑工业出版社出版、发行（北京西郊百万庄）
各地新华书店、建筑书店经销
北京锋尚制版有限公司制版
北京方嘉彩色印刷有限责任公司印刷
*
开本：889×1194毫米　1/20　印张：5⅗　字数：151千字
2016年1月第一版　2016年1月第一次印刷
定价：48.00元
ISBN 978 – 7 – 112 – 18250 – 3
　　　（27381）

ACKNOWLEDGEMENTS
致谢

Harvard Graduate School of Design Faculty

Kongjian Yu, Professor of Landscape Architecture (PKU)

Adrian Blackwell, Visiting Assistant Professor of Landscape

Architecture (University of Waterloo)

Stephen Ervin, Lecturer, Director of Information Technology

(Harvard GSD)

Editing and Translation

Yujun Yin, (MLA AP & MARCH2) Teaching Assistant (Harvard GSD)

Wei Li (Beida—Harvard Ecological Urbanism Collaboration)

哈佛大学设计学院（GSD）

俞孔坚	北京大学景观设计教授
阿德里安·布莱克韦尔	哈佛大学设计学院客座教授，滑铁卢大学景观设计学助理教授
斯蒂芬·欧文	哈佛大学设计学院信息技术学院副院长

编译

| 尹毓俊 | 哈佛大学设计学院助教 |
| 李薇 | 北京大学–哈佛大学生态城市联合实验室 |

Harvard Graduate School of Design Students

Benjamin Scheerbarth

Cynthia Dehlavi

Erin Hannes

Frank Refuerzo

Jisoo Kim

Jacob Sippy

Juan Reyna Monreal

Omar Davis

Susan Nguyen

Shanji Li

Simon Willett

Zander Hannes

哈佛大学设计学院　学生

本杰明·舍尔巴尔特

辛西娅·德拉维

埃林·汉内斯

弗朗克

金智秀

雅各布·西皮

胡安·雷纳·蒙雷亚尔

奥马尔·戴维斯

苏珊·源

李善姬

西蒙·威利特

桑德尔·汉内斯

Contents
目录

INTRODUCTION

课程介绍

China's Dream: a new urbanization

China's "reform and open" period, which began in the late 1970s and accelerated in the early 1990s, has unleashed an unprecedented process of urbanization. The development of land has had a central role in the reform economy, as both a key infrastructure for other forms of production and as a key commodity in its own right. It has precipitated an equally unprecedented migration of people from rural areas into cities, and at the same time created serious ecological problems.

The speed of transformation has produced enormous mismatches between the supply and demand of housing, with much of it sitting empty for investment, while migrants live in crowded factory dormitories or urban villages, creating an urban environment of economic polarization. At the same time, the current design of cities exacerbates the global ecological crisis. Water, air and soil have been dangerously polluted, farmland is disappearing, and disastrous flooding is a yearly occurrence.

These problems are evident to commentators around the world, and they sit at the forefront of concerns that the Chinese Central Government is struggling to address. In response to these growing problems, new policies call for "New Urbanization", to replace the "Old Urbanization", which has been characterized as socially unequal and ecologically unsustainable. New Urbanization should support for social equity, build an ecocivilization and produce a flourishing culture. As a step in this direction, the idea of landscape security patterns, a concept developed by Kongjian Yu in his dissertation at the GSD has adopted as a national strategy.

中国梦：新的城镇化模式

中国的改革开放政策始于20世纪70年代，并于90年代开始大规模地影响中国的城市化进程。土地的使用权商品化及其关键性生产基础设施的地位，使其在经济转型中发挥了核心的作用。这个过程伴随着规模空前的农村人口向城市转移，同时引发了严峻的生态问题。

过快的城市发展和转型，导致了居住空间的供给和需求之间巨大的错位。一方面，大量住房因用于投资目的而空置，而另一方面大量的新移民却拥挤在工厂宿舍和城中村中，城市环境突显出经济两极化。另外，当前的城市规划和设计也加剧了全球生态危机：水体、空气和土地被严重污染，耕地逐渐消失，灾害性的洪水常年造访。

这些生态环境问题不仅引发了全世界的关注，也是中国中央政府正竭力解决的头等问题。作为应对，最新的国家政策提出了以"新型城镇化"替代社会发展不平衡和生态不可持续的"旧城镇化"之路，以此促进社会公平，建设生态文明并推动文化繁荣。为了实现这个目标，俞孔坚教授在哈佛大学博士论文中提出的"景观生态安全格局"的概念，受到国家领导人重视，并把它提升为一项国家战略。

本课程设计以景观作为主要的工具来重新思考城市设计中的关键问题。这种规划策略建立在俞教授的"反规划"理论基础上，即以生态基础设施引导城市发展。中国

This studio considers landscape architecture as a key tool for rethinking essential processes of urban design. It will build on Yu's theorization of negative planning as a strategy for letting ecological infrastructure lead urban development. The Chinese urban revolution has severed social and ecological fluxes that once allowed for the healthy functioning of both social and natural systems. The aim of the studio is to analyze these systems in order to consider how a new process of urbanization might proceed through the reconnection of these damaged social and ecological systems.

目前的城市化截断了维持健康社会和自然系统功能所仰赖的社会和生态流，而本课程设计的目标便是对这些社会和自然系统进行分析，并通过恢复这些被破坏的系统间联系来为中国的城镇化进程提供一种新模式。

BUILDING A NEW COMMUNIST COUNRTYSIDE-PROPAGANDA DRAWING
建设社会主义新农村宣传画

大寨村　资料来源：黄国平收集
Dazhai Village　Source: Collection of Huang Guoping

FARMERS IMMIGRANT INTO THE METROPOLIS AREA AFTER 1990S
20世纪90年代大量农村居民入城工作

THE FACT BEHIND HIGH SPEED URBANIZATION
高速城市化背后被破坏的生态环境和自然灾害

SITUATION

According to Beijing's 2004-2020 Master Plan, the metropolitan region will evolve toward a polycentric structure, with "two axes, two belts and multiple centers". The two axes run east to west and north to south, crossing at central Beijing. The two belts are the western ecological belt and the eastern development belt.

Multiple centers refer to points of density and commercial activity within the broader field of mixed-use urban development. Haidian district is located on the northern section of the western ecological belt and is noted for its educational resources and high-tech and scientific research developments. The official Haidian district plan calls for the expansion of these specialized industries, coupled with residential new towns, and the preservation of important open-space and ecological reserves. The Nansha River runs through the town of Shangzhuang in the northern part of Haidian District. It is a tributary of Wenyu River one of the most significant waterways feeding Beijing. The total length of the river is 21km, while the catchment area covers 220 sq km.

This area is characterized by a seemingly random mix of urban and rural spaces. Aerial photography clearly illustrates that it is formed as a checkerboard of alternating and diverse uses that seem to have little connection to one another, from rural farmland to urban villages, or from relocation housing to high tech and even creative industries. In order to understand this condition better the studio examined its diverse ecological conditions, its rural practices, and its urban incursions, in order to map the problems and potentials that the site offers for urban life.

Within this area environmental challenges include urban flooding and water pollution. Mono-functional engineering, such as channelization and damming have brought fundamental changes to the urban hydrological process and functions, such that the river and its tributaries no longer have the capacity for flood control or self-purification through ecological processes, leading to the ongoing degradation of

现状

北京城市总体规划（2004－2020）提出构建"两轴—两带—多中心"的新城市空间格局。"两轴"指在北京中心交会的东西轴和南北轴，"两带"则指的是西部生态带和东部发展带。

多中心是指城区中混合功能的高密度发展区域。海淀区位于西部发展带的北面，集中了北京市的高等教育资源，是高新技术产业基地和科研机构聚集区。海淀区的发展规划要求进一步扩展这些特色产业，新建住宅区域的同时保留重要的开阔地和生态保护区。南沙河流经海淀区北部的上庄镇，是北京重要的饮水水源温榆河的一个支流，全长21公里，流域覆盖220平方公里。

这块区域像是城市和农村的随机组合。从卫星图像上很明显地看到，其内部用地类型像棋盘格一样交替、混合分布，但各自间又似乎缺乏联系，比如耕地旁边是城中村，农民安置房又紧挨着科技园甚至创意产业园。为了深入了解这种发展现状，本课程设计将通过研究不同的生态环境、农村发展实践和城市扩张的情况来揭示南沙河城市化过程中的问题和潜力。

在这个区域中，环境挑战包括城市防洪和治理水污染。单一功能的工程设计，如开挖泄洪渠道和建立防洪堤等做法已从根本上改变了城市的天然水文过程及功能，河道及支流慢慢丧失了其生态防洪和自我净化的能力，导致区域生态持续恶化。

城中村本是城市外围的郊区居住地，随着城市的扩张在过去的20年里逐渐变为农民工聚集区，但这里的居住环境无法满足他们对清洁饮用水和卫生设施的要求。海淀区北部的新房建设包括奢华的别墅区，外来专业人士的经济

the region's ecology.

Urban villages, formerly rural settlements beyond the city have been gradually connected to urban sprawl and transformed over the past two decades into cramped accommodation for migrant workers. In their current condition these villages are unable to meet their residents' needs for clean water and sanitation services. New housing in northern Haidian spans a broad economic spectrum from luxury villas, to affordable suburban neighborhoods for professional migrants to Beijing, to relocation housing for downtown residents. In each case these new neighborhoods, contribute to increased infrastructure demand while consuming valuable farmland. The emerging tourist industry in the region, which includes "agritainment" and vacation villages, contributes to the water pollution by discharging sewage into reservoirs and rivers.

In the face of these complex problems the studio proposed the design of a mixed use settlement along the Nansha river, starting from the concept of negative planning. Students used ecological infrastructure to reconnect fluxes of water, food and populations, in order to design the new landscape and architectural forms of a "New Commune" which would be socially equitable, ecologically sustainable and culturally flourishing.

适用房，以及拆迁居民的安置房，吸引着不同经济水平的群体。可以预见，满足任何一种社会群体对基础设施的需求都必然要消耗珍贵的耕地。另外，这个区域新兴的旅游业，尤其是农家乐和度假村，常常直接向水库和河流排放污水，加剧了对水资源的污染。

针对这些复杂的问题，课程设计提出从"反规划"的概念出发，为南沙河区域设计一个兼容不同发展需求的方案。学生们将利用生态基础设施来为水、食物和人重新建立联系，通过一种全新的景观和建筑形式来建立一个社会公平、生态可持续以及文化繁荣的新社区。

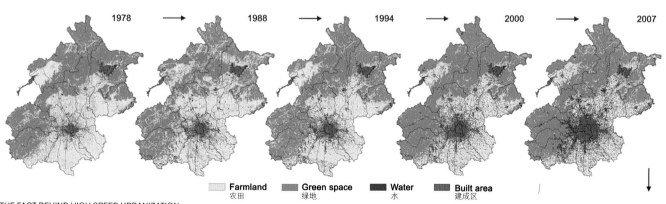

| Farmland 农田 | Green space 绿地 | Water 水 | Built area 建成区 |

THE FACT BEHIND HIGH SPEED URBANIZATION
城市化背后被破坏的生态环境和自然灾害

9

STRATEGY

The studio explored the design potentials of Kongjian Yu's strategy of "negative planning" as a method for designing urban landscapes. Negative planning begins by examining and leveraging existing conditions of urban and rural space, in opposition to positive planning which tends to impose novel structures on existing sites. Negative planning has four key dimensions:

1. Negative planning is first of all a fundamental critique of modernist planning methods that focus primarily on population projection and civil engineering solutions to urban problems.

2. It operates by inverting the normative hierarchies of planning, which posit built form as the primary organizing system of urban space. Instead affirming socio-natural networks as the foundation of urbanization.

3. Negative planning locates human and non-human actors on the same plane, privileging three existing systems as primary elements of any new urban plan: a) abiotic – geologic, hydrologic, and climatic -systems; b) biotic systems including both animal and vegetal communities; c) cultural systems incorporating infrastructure, buildings, public spaces, transportation and energy networks, recreational, commercial, educational and other human-built systems.

4. This broad understanding of what makes up the urban, forces designers into inter-disciplinary collaborations that necessarily acknowledge the temporal unfolding of urbanism, as a series of possible scenarios, promoting the understanding of site as a situation, as an intersection of spatial and temporal forces.

策略

课程设计试图探索将俞教授的"反规划"策略作为一种城市景观设计方法的可能性。正规划通常是在现有空间中强行植入一个新的结构，而"反规划"正相反，它要求先探索和利用现有的城市和乡村空间。"反规划"有四个关键点：

1. "反规划"首先反对只通过人口预测和市政设施建设来寻求城市问题解决方案的现代规划方法。

2. 它倒转标准性的规划程序，不再以建筑结构作为城市空间首要组织系统，而是把社会和自然网络作为城镇化的基础。

3. "反规划"对人与非人的因素同样重视，在任何城市规划中都把三个现存系统作为考虑的首要因素：a）非生物系统–地质；水文和气候系统；b）生物系统，同时包括动植物系统；c）文化系统，结合了基础设施、建筑、公共空间、交通和能源网络、休闲、商业、教育和其他人类建立的系统。

4. 用更广阔深远的角度去理解城市的构成，有利于推动城市设计师以跨学科的方式合作，让人认识到城镇化多样的可能性。一个特定的场地，不仅富含当下现状的信息，也集中体现了时间和空间力量的交集。

Scenario 2: Green infrastructure within the city: urban growth based on minimum EI.

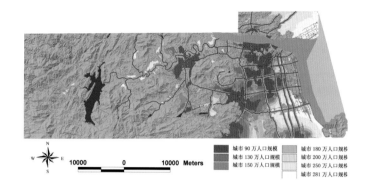

Scenario 4: Garden suburban: urban growth based on ideal EI.

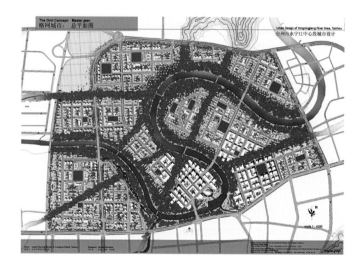

NEGATIVE PLANNING
反规划理念案例

METHODOLOGY

The studio investigated the site through a strategy of negative planning at multiple scales, following the method outlined below:

1. Students began by studying the fluxes that circulate on the site at different scales. The class was divided into six groups of two, with each group focusing on a different material flux along the Nansha River:

(1) Water - Hydrology
(2) Food/Nutrients - Agriculture
(3) Species - Habitat
(4) People - Built form
(5) Energy - Infrastructure
(6) Economy - Land use

2. After analyzing this system, students followed a process of selection or curation, finding dimensions of the existing (broken) system of fluxes that could be preserved and/or altered to serve as structural elements for a new design. Within case studies and precedents of negative planning this often highlights hydrological systems, but students were encouraged to find these structures within their specific subject of investigation, aollowing contemporary patterns of development to be grounded within the site's social history and ecological systems.

3. Next students added strategic infrastructures and built forms to the found system of fluxes, in order to support healthy patterns of urbanization. These new elements learned from local practices and precedents as well as new and globalized technologies. Both the urban design and landscape architectural dimensions of the resulting project were evaluated to see how these systems might produce a "new commune."

方法

本课程设计按照"反规划"的理念，通过以下的方法从多个尺度对此区域进行研究：

1. 学生们首先研究在不同尺度上经过此区域的流系统。学生分成6个小组，每组两人，每组分别研究南沙河的一个物质流：

（1）水–水文系统
（2）食物/营养–农业
（3）物种–栖息地
（4）人–建筑形式
（5）能量– 基础设施
（6）经济–用地

2. 分析了这些系统后，学生们需选取其中一个现存（被破坏）的流系统，以保护或改变此系统作为新设计中的结构性要素。以往的案例研究和"反规划"先例往往以水文系统为主体，但我们鼓励学生为他们选中的不同研究主体进行系统结构的剖析，把握好这些后才能确保当前发展规划能与此区域的社会历史和生态系统相适应。

3. 接着学生们要为选中的系统添加策略性的基础设施或建筑形式，来形成城镇化的健康模式。新添的这些元素可以借鉴本地的实践经验、以往的或是新颖的例子、全球范围内的新技术。项目完成后，我们会同时从城市规划和景观建筑两个角度来评估这些系统如何能帮助建立一个新型社区。

4. The final stage of the design process imagined future growth scenarios for the site. Negative planning is in part about setting specific parameters as a framework for future change and evolution. It is a logic that engages uncertainty and adaptability. The studio speculated on how designed infrastructures would allow a vibrant city to evolve in the future.

4. 设计的最后一个阶段是预测该社区的未来发展情境。"反规划"通过设定几个特定的参数形成未来城市发展和演化的框架，给不确定性和适应性留出了充分的空间。本课程设计将大胆地预测这些设想中的基础设施如何能促进城市的未来发展。

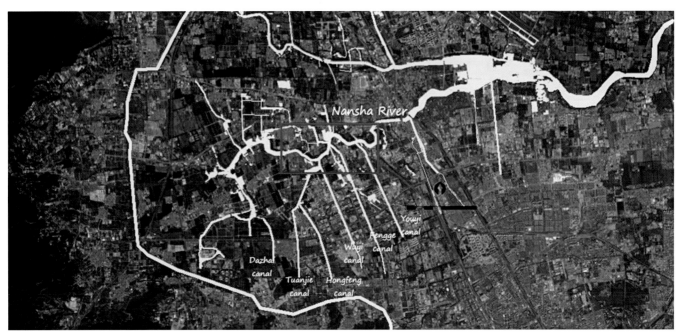

NANSHA RIVER WATERSHED
南沙河流域

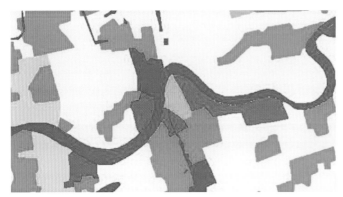

1993 NANSHAHE LANDUSE
1993年南沙河片区用地

2010 NANSHAHE LANDUSE
2010年南沙河片区用地

PROJECTS AND SCALES

The Studio examined the site at various scales of analysis and design, through five parts of one term project divided into 2 assignments, one analytical, the second based in design.

Assignment one was group analysis project, consisting of two parts designed to prepare students for the design proposal:

a) Mapping Fluxes was a remote topological examination of the site through the lens of the group's chosen system of flux at the scales of Beijing, Haidian, and the Nansha River.

b) Experiencing Fluxes was detailed typological analysis of the onsite material conditions of the site, produced during the site visit to Beijing, Haidian, and the Nansha River.

Assignment 2 was a single design project done in three parts:

a) Reweaving (Topology) was an initial design experiment completed before leaving for Beijing. It allowed students to workshop ideas for reconnecting the fluxes of the Nansha River with designers and officials during the trip to Beijing.

b) Typological Machines was a group or individual project that proposed a detailed design for the modifications to the overall flows described in topological reweaving.

c) A New Commune was a detailed urban proposal for one urban village done individually or in groups. The design focused on the overall plan of a new commune connecting topological ideas to typological propositions.

STUDIO OBJECTIVES

The objectives of the studio were to: (1) Develop regional and site-scale landscape and urban strategies (scenarios) based on analysis of the ecological and socio-economic context, using "negative planning" principles; (2) Develop alternative landscape and urban design proposals at a site-scale that respond to these regional development scenarios, and engage China's aspirations for a new urbanization.

项目和尺度

课程在不同尺度上对该区域进行分析和设计，一个学期的项目任务为两个作业，一个侧重分析，一个侧重设计，总共涵盖5部分内容。

作业一：团队分析,包括两部分，为作业二的设计提案做准备：

a）图绘流：通过远程拓扑绘制出每个组所选择的流系统在北京、海淀区和南沙河三个尺度的基本情况。

b）体验流：在对北京、海淀区和南沙河进行实地考察的时候，对场地的物质状况做出详细的类型分析。

作业二：独立设计项目，由三部分组成

a）再织流：在离开北京之前必须完成的首个设计实验。学生们在北京实地考察的时候将同设计师和当地官员一起合作讨论，对如何再织流进行思考。

b）类型工具：团队或独立设计项目，是对上个阶段的想法做出的整体和深化设计。

c）新型社区：团队或独立设计项目，给出城中村城市化的详细方案，重点在这个新型社区的整体规划如何使拓扑结构和类型相互契合。

课程设计目标

（1）依据"反规划"理念，在生态和社会经济环境的分析基础上提出地方和区域的景观及城市发展策略；

（2）响应区域发展规划蓝图，为地方提供创造性的景观和城市发展策略，为中国的新型城镇化提供示范。

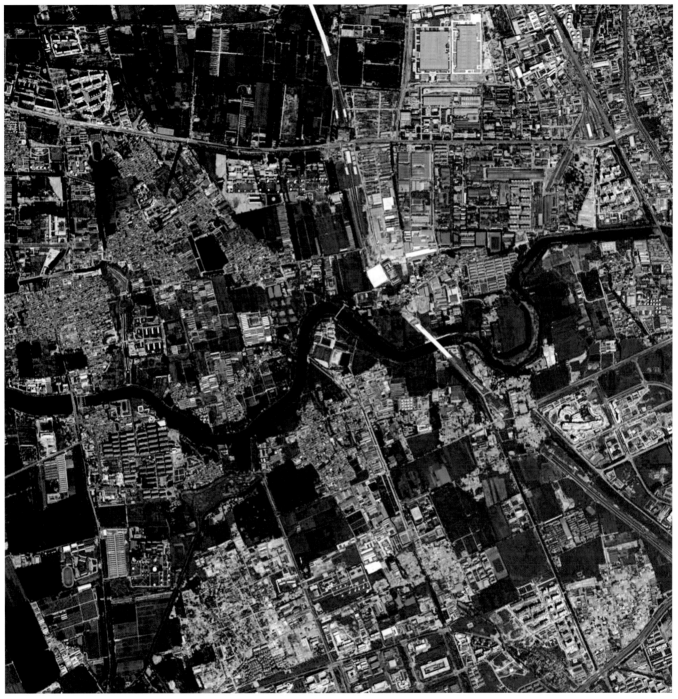

AERIAL VIEW OF LAND-USEMOSAIC
土地使用现状卫星图

WATER SYSTEM-BEIJING
水系统分析

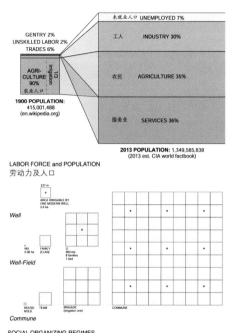

UNEMPLOYED 7%

GENTRY 2%
UNSKILLED LABOR 2%
TRADES 6%

工人 INDUSTRY 30%

AGRI-
CULTURE
90%
农业人口

1/3 irrigation

农民 AGRICULTURE 35%

1900 POPULATION:
415,001,488
(en.wikipedia.org)

服务业 SERVICES 36%

2013 POPULATION: 1,349,585,838
(2013 est. CIA world factbook)

LABOR FORCE and POPULATION
劳动力及人口

Well

237 m
AREA IRRIGABLE BY
ONE MODERN WELL
5.6 ha

MU
0.06 ha

FAMILY
(CLAN)

900 mu
8 families
1 field

Well-Field

HOUSE-
HOLD

TEAM

BRIGADE
(Irrigation Unit)

COMMUNE

Commune

SOCIAL ORGANIZING REGIMES
水资源的社会分配

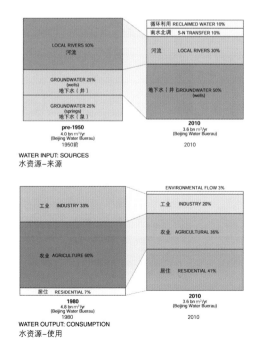

LOCAL RIVERS 50%
河流

循环利用 RECLAIMED WATER 10%
南水北调 S-N TRANSFER 10%

河流 LOCAL RIVERS 30%

GROUNDWATER 25%
(wells)
地下水（井）

地下水（井）GROUNDWATER 50%
(wells)

GROUNDWATER 25%
(springs)
地下水（泉）

pre-1950
4.0 bn m³/yr
(Beijing Water Buerau)
1950前

2010
3.6 bn m³/yr
(Beijing Water Buerau)
2010

WATER INPUT: SOURCES
水资源－来源

ENVIRONMENTAL FLOW 3%

工业 INDUSTRY 33%

工业 INDUSTRY 20%

农业 AGRICULTURAL 36%

农业 AGRICULTURE 60%

居住 RESIDENTIAL 41%

居住 RESIDENTIAL 7%

1980
4.8 bn m³/yr
(Beijing Water Buerau)
1980

2010
3.6 bn m³/yr
(Beijing Water Buerau)
2010

WATER OUTPUT: CONSUMPTION
水资源－使用

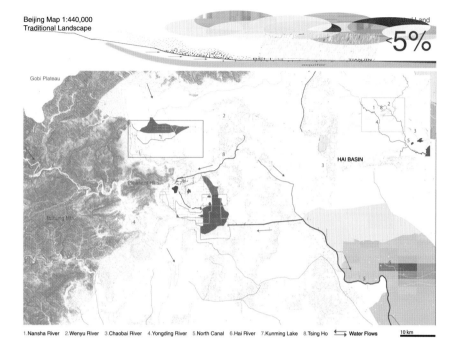

Beijing Map 1:440,000
Traditional Landscape

Land
<5%

Gobi Plateau

HAI BASIN

Pleasant Hills

Taihang Mts.

1.Nansha River 2.Wenyu River 3.Chaobai River 4.Yongding River 5.North Canal 6.Hai River 7.Kunming Lake 8.Tsing Ho → Water Flows 10 km

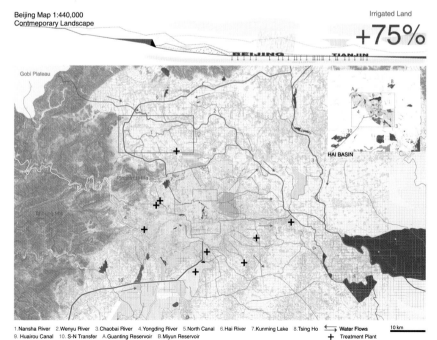

Beijing Map 1:440,000
Contmeporary Landscape

Irrigated Land
+75%

BEIJING TIANJIN

Gobi Plateau

HAI BASIN

Pleasant Hills

Taihang Mts.

1.Nansha River 2.Wenyu River 3.Chaobai River 4.Yongding River 5.North Canal 6.Hai River 7.Kunming Lake 8.Tsing Ho → Water Flows 10 km
9. Huairou Canal 10. S-N Transfer A.Guanting Reservoir B.Miyun Reservoir + Treatment Plant

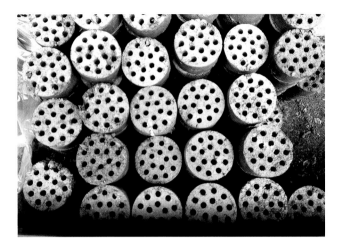

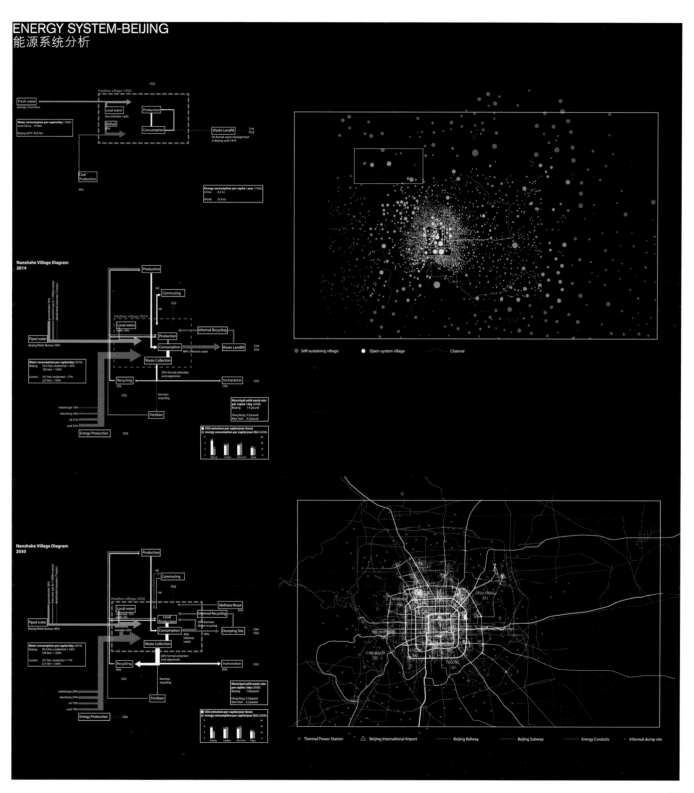

Self-sustaining village   **Open-system village**   Channel

+ Thermal Power Station   △ Beijing International Airport   Beijing Railway   Beijing Subway   Energy Conduits   Informal dump site

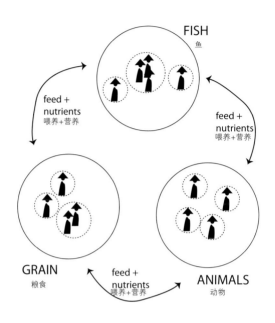

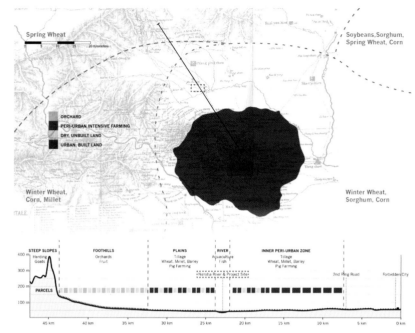

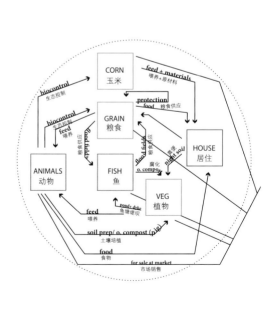

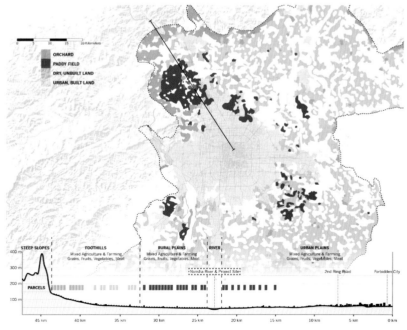

ECONOMY / LAND USE-BEIJING
经济/用地系统分析

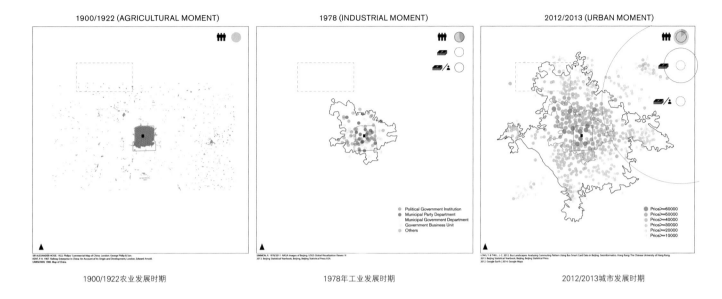

1900/1922 (AGRICULTURAL MOMENT)

1978 (INDUSTRIAL MOMENT)

2012/2013 (URBAN MOMENT)

1900/1922农业发展时期

1978年工业发展时期

2012/2013城市发展时期

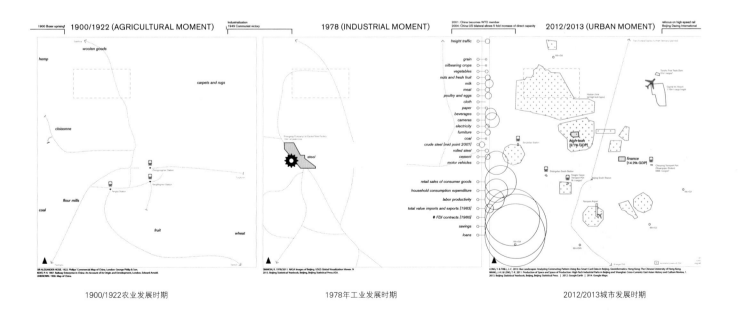

1900/1922 (AGRICULTURAL MOMENT)

1978 (INDUSTRIAL MOMENT)

2012/2013 (URBAN MOMENT)

1900/1922农业发展时期

1978年工业发展时期

2012/2013城市发展时期

PEOPLE + BUILT FORM-BEIJING
人+建筑类型系统

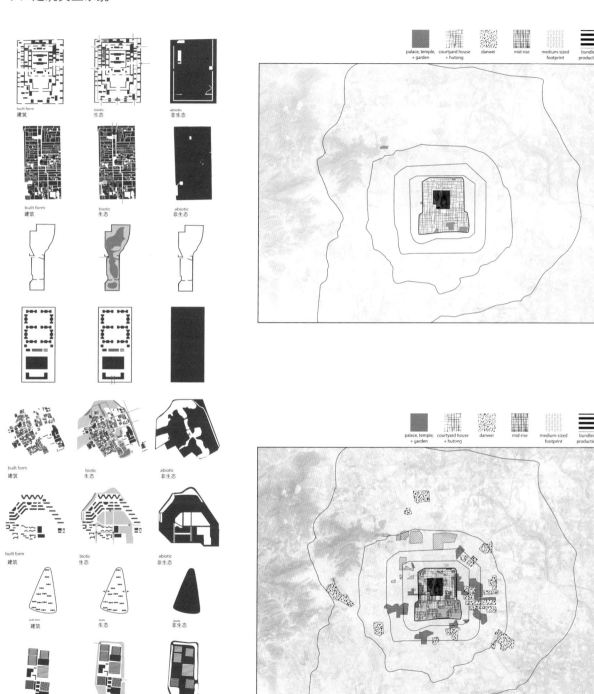

built form
建筑

biotic
生态

abiotic
非生态

palace, temple, + garden | courtyard house + hutong | danwei | mid-rise | medium-sized footprint | bundled production | hi-rise | campus

SPECIES-BEIJING
物种系统

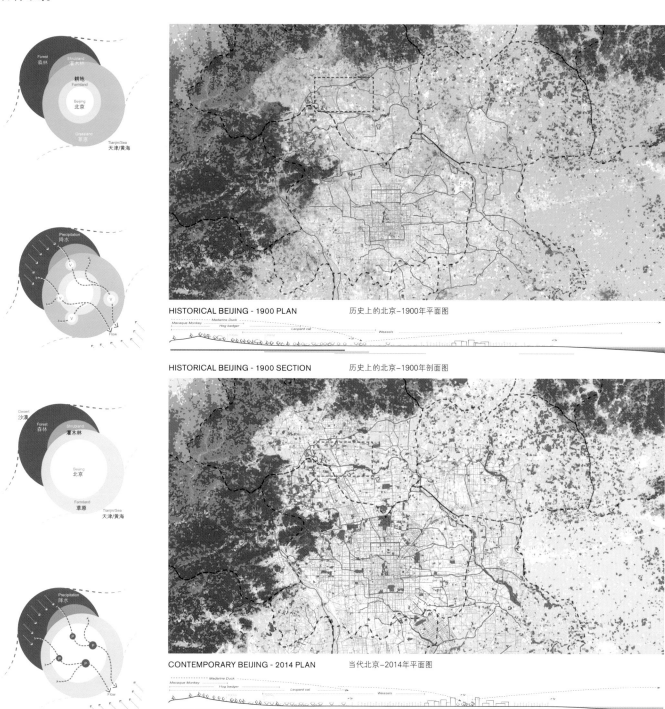

HISTORICAL BEIJING - 1900 PLAN   历史上的北京–1900年平面图

HISTORICAL BEIJING - 1900 SECTION   历史上的北京–1900年剖面图

CONTEMPORARY BEIJING - 2014 PLAN   当代北京–2014年平面图

CONTEMPORARY BEIJING - 2014 SECTION   当代北京–2014年剖面图

URBAN ISLANDS-GROUNDWATER SEA

Jacob Sippy
Simon Willett

In order to combat Beijing's sustained water scarcity crisis, the proposal suggests an innovative water banking strategy around its peri-urban edge. Roughly coinciding with the sixth circumferintial highway, this "blue ring" will form a physical urban growth boundary while simultaneously metamorphosizing the existing landscape of villages and marginalized land uses. Composed of hydro-districts centered on natural and man-made watercourses, the ring will collect and clean natural rainwater flowing toward Bohai Bay from the western mountains and greywater run off from the impervious footprint of the metropolois. These districts incorporate and intensify existing settlement to maintain greenfields for infiltration and evapotranspiration, creating a framework for hydrological restoration that structures proximate, complimentary land uses defined by their respective water consumption requirements. This linked archipelago of urban islands will move particularly noxious entities, like heavy industry, upland to free up land for both water banking and future residential expansion. The new development strategy thus maintains in situ urban fabric and culture while new "meteorite" developments in each respective village comprising the archipelago will suggest future densities and introduce highly water efficient communal structures. Several new typologies are introduced which build upon the panorama of traditional and vernacular forms, particularly the courtyard as both an autonomous and urban entitiy. Landscape is transformed through the cutting of deep, artificial wetlands, once abundant in the area, and naturalized channels which will treat water while simultaneously mollifying flash floods.

城市岛屿与地下水的海洋

为了解决北京的水资源短缺问题，本方案提出一个环北京城郊的创新储水方案。这个"蓝色水环"与北京新建的六环道路基本重合，构成北京城区扩张的物理边界，同时与现有的乡村景观和城市边缘用地有机结合。蓝色水环由有水的区域连接而成，尤其是自然与人工的河道，它能够用以收集并过滤从西山流入渤海湾的雨水以及都市生活产生的大量地表灰水。这个区域将保存并加强现有的居住区，保留尚未开发的区域以利于水分渗透和蒸腾蒸发，形成一个水系统修复框架。这个框架的建立会充分考虑每个区的用水需求及其界定的周边用地性质。这个城市岛屿的布局需要迁出一些重点污染源，如重工业，到更外围的区域，空出的用地将作为水存储和将来的住宅开发之用。这种新型的城市发展策略不仅保存了该地现有的城市肌理和文化，同时在每个岛屿中发展起来的卫星城镇将在未来发展新的城市密度的同时实现水资源的高效利用。该提案引入了数种建立在传统和本土灵感上的建筑类型，尤其是院落这种既自主又与城市紧密联系的形式。在景观的改造上，切出了较深的人工湿地来恢复过去的天然湿地景观，修建了自然化的渠道，有助于水的净化同时缓和暴洪的侵袭。

CURRENT INPUTS AND OUTPUTS
水资源供排

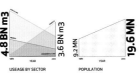

HUMAN INFLUENCE ON WATER IN BEIJING
居民对水资源的影响

HISTORIC AND CURRENT RAINFALL FLOWS
地表水的历史及现状

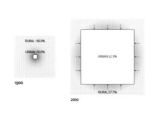

SOCIAL IRRIGATION PARADIGMS
人工灌溉的范例

EXISTING RAINFALL POTENTIAL FLOWS
地表水现状及潜在径流

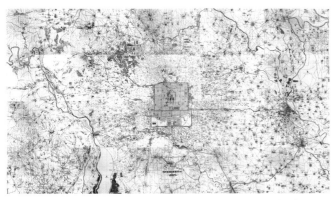

MAP OF BEIJING IN 1900 ILLUSTRATING AN ARCHIPELAGO OF URBAN NODES
1900年北京城与周边城镇的断裂状态

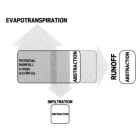

URBAN POPULATION IN CHINA
城市人口

PROPOSED RAINFALL FLOWS WITH
DOUBLE THE POPULATION
提案–组织雨水径流及加密人口密度

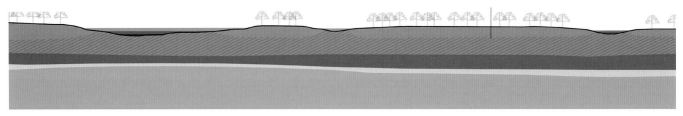

HISTORIC HYDROLOGICAL SECTION SHOWING ABUNDANCE
历史剖面–北京丰富的水资源

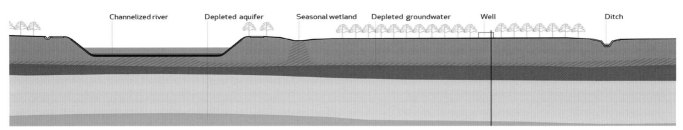

EXISTING HYDROLOGICAL SECTION SHOWING SCARCITY
现状剖面–北京短缺的水资源

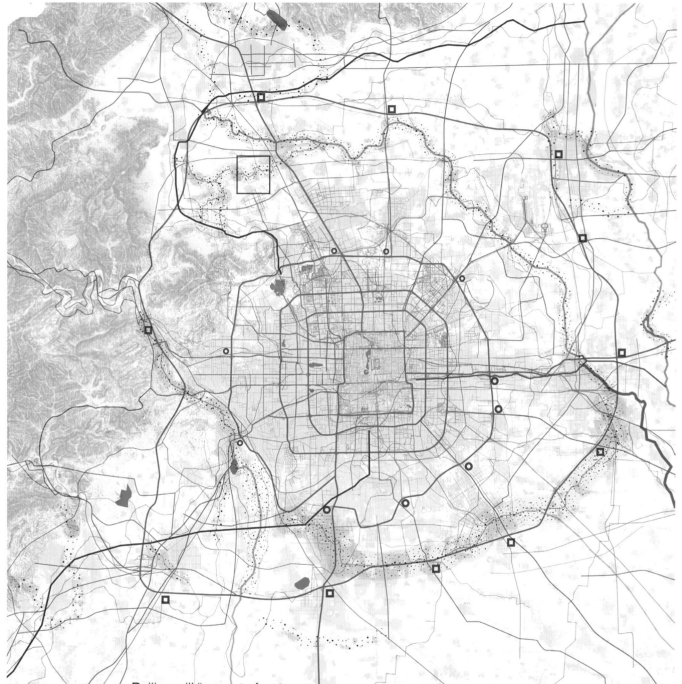

Some are speculating that Beijing will "run out of water within...ten years." Aware of this, the government continues to construct reservoirs and canals up to thousands of kilometers away. Unfortunately, new reservoirs are merely delaying actions as neighboring provinces are being drained of water as well.

(Water Digest, July 20, 2010)

WATER BANKING CORRIDORS CREATE A PHYSICAL URBAN GROWTH BOUNDARY
存水廊道—城市发展的物理边界

0   10 km

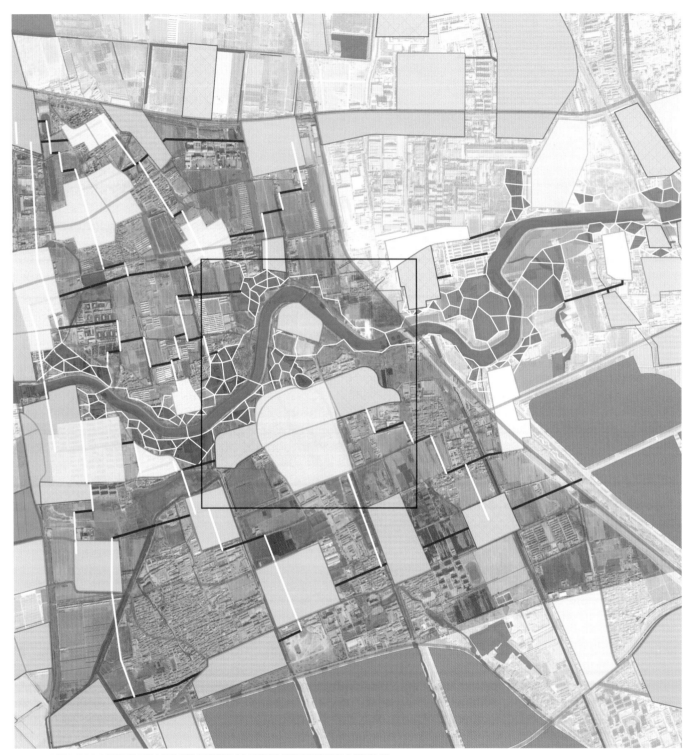

SITE PLAN OF HYDRO-DISTRICT AND LAND USE ARCHIPELAGO WITHIN THE BLUE RING CORRIDOR
基地平面-蓝色水环内的水系统及城市用地

0   800 m

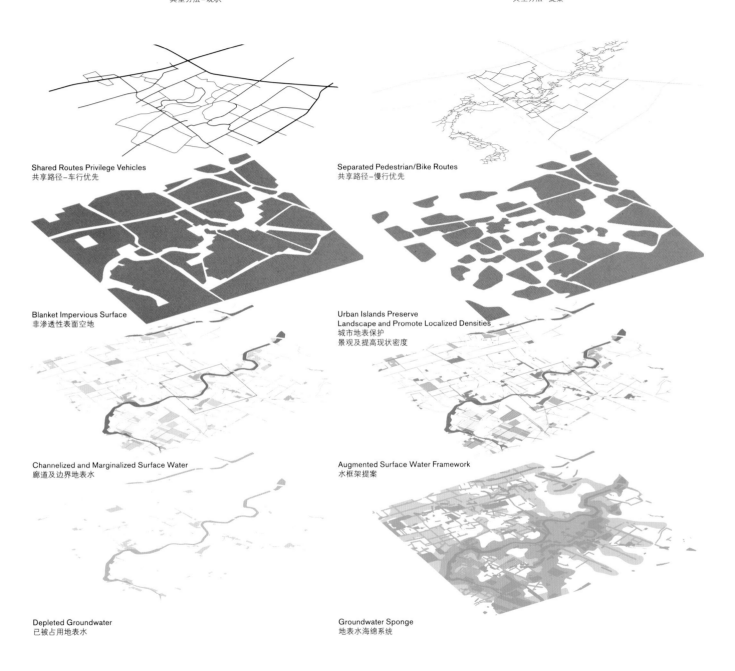

TOPOLOGICAL LAYERS - EXISTING
典型分层–现状

TOPOLOGICAL LAYERS - PROPOSED
典型分层–提案

Shared Routes Privilege Vehicles
共享路径–车行优先

Separated Pedestrian/Bike Routes
共享路径–慢行优先

Blanket Impervious Surface
非渗透性表面空地

Urban Islands Preserve
Landscape and Promote Localized Densities
城市地表保护
景观及提高现状密度

Channelized and Marginalized Surface Water
廊道及边界地表水

Augmented Surface Water Framework
水框架提案

Depleted Groundwater
已被占用地表水

Groundwater Sponge
地表水海绵系统

NEW SUMMER PALACE
避暑山庄–自然与人工集影
Source: The United States Library of
Congress's Geography & Map Division
资料来源：美国国会图书馆地理地图部收藏

BEIJING BASELINE
北京标准

DENSITY	FAR/FSI	UNITS/ha
73 p/ha	1.0	27

XIYUHE 2010 NEED
1.4 MN M3/YR
西御河2010年需求

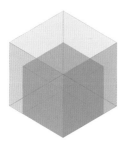

XIYUHE 2040 NEED
2.7 MN M3/YR
西御河2040年需求

2040 POTENTIAL RAINFALL
ABSTRACTION 2.2~3.4 MN M3/YR
2040年预计雨量

HAKKA TULOU, FUJIAN By Wangying
土楼 摄影：王颖

OPEN TOULOU CONTAINS PUBLIC SPACE
土楼开放空间参考

DENSITY	FAR/FSI	UNITS/ha
234 p/ha	1.3	56

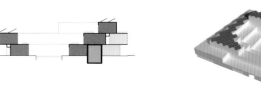

VERNACULAR TOWN, CHENGKAN
By Liwei
安徽呈坎 摄影：李薇

RIVERSIDE REDEVELOPMENT
GENERATES PUBLIC ACCESS
河岸的重新规划–增加公共可达性

DENSITY	FAR/FSI	UNITS/ha
133 p/ha	0.6	52

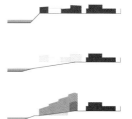

SHINONOME CANAL COURT BLOCK,
TOKYO (RIKEN YAMAMOTO) By Liujia
东京东云站河居住区 摄影：刘佳

VERTICAL HUTONG ATOP A
PUBLIC ROOFSCAPE
垂直胡同–公共的竖向公共空间

DENSITY	FAR/FSI	UNITS/ha
227 p/ha	3.2	73

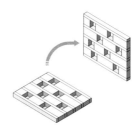

JU'ER HUTONG REHABILITATION,
BEIJING (WU LIANGYONG) By
ZhangYan and Fang Ke
菊儿胡同 摄影：方可、章岩

MAT TEXTURE INFILL ENSURES
ENVIRONMENTAL QUALITY WITH DENSITY
绿色填充–密度与居住质量并存

DENSITY	FAR/FSI	UNITS/ha
264 p/ha	1.3	89

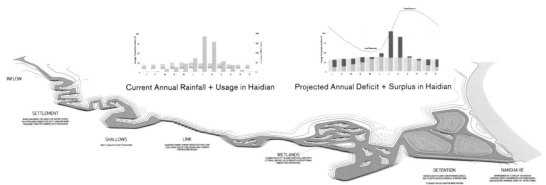

Current Annual Rainfall + Usage in Haidian

Projected Annual Deficit + Surplus in Haidian

REIMAGINE TREATMENT TYPOLOGIES
水组织及过滤提案

IMPERIAL APPROACH TO WATER
皇家园林的亲水性
Source: Collection of La Biblio-
thèqve Nationale de France
资料来源：法国国家图书馆收藏

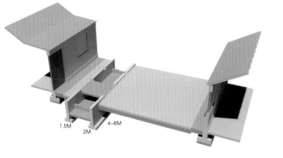

FEEDER TYPE RUNNEL FOR STORMWATER MANAGEMENT
灌溉式组织排水系统

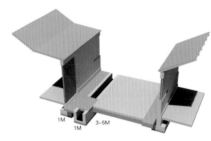

ALLEY TYPE RUNNEL FOR DRAINAGE
廊道式组织排水系统

**DIVERSE FORMS OF
ENGAGEMENT By Liwei**
多样的水空间　摄影：李薇

**WATER INTEGRATED INTO
DAILY LIFE By Liwei**
水空间渗透到日常生活　摄影：李薇

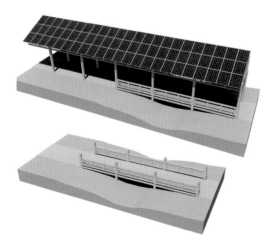

**BRIDGE TYPES INCLUDE COVERED (E-W) AND OPEN (N-S)
BOARDWALKS**
桥梁系统

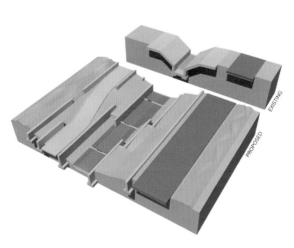

IMPROVED CHANNEL FOR ENHANCED ACCESS AND INFILTRATION
改良式渗透水廊道

**WATER AS THE PUBLIC SPACE
By Liwei**
水公共空间　摄影：李薇

**VERNACULAR WALLS AND
BRIDGES By Liwei**
水空间中的桥与墙　摄影：李薇

SITE PLAN OF HYDRO-DISTRICT AND LAND USE ARCHIPELAGO WITHIN THE BLUE RING CORRIDOR
基地平面–蓝色水环内的水系统及城市用地

THE PONDS
THE PROMONTORY
THE WETLANDS

THE WETLANDS

THE PONDS

XIYUHE VILLAGE DURING THE DRY SEASON
西御河村–枯水季

XIYUHE VILLAGE DURING THE RAINY SEASON
西御河村–丰水季

SCHEME PERSPECTIVE
水环境提案

CITY SECTION SHOWING PROPOSED IMPROVEMENTS TO THE EXISTING URBAN FABRIC TOWARD A REDUCTION OF IMPERVIOUS SURFACE, AN INCREASE IN DENSITY, AND A BETTER QUALITY OF LIFE
城市剖面–通过整体规划提升地表水资源的收集及对地下水位的补藏，与此同时提高了城市的目的及生活质量

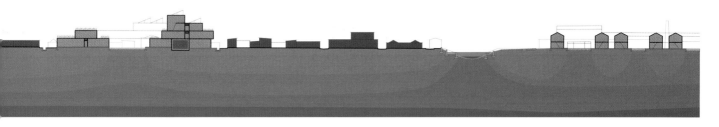

0   400 m

ARTICULATED DISPERSION

On a look at humans as part of the species continuum

Jisoo Kim

Juan Reyna Monrreal

As the political capital of China, Beijing possesses a rich urban history that has left an indelible footprint in the landscape. Once a thriving valley surrounded by forests, shrublands, grasslands, and wetlands; the accelerated rate of "modernization" since the beginning of the 20th century has severed the historical linkages between man and nature. Articulated Dispersion attempts to provide a regional solution to the problem of urban and agricultural sprawl. The project concentrates development and production into highly-dense nodes that allow for natural systems and ecological services to be restored on-site and comprise the main infrastructure upon which a new model of sustainable city is constructed.

Articulated dispersion positions a framework for examining humans as a single component of a much larger species continuum. The project's analysis methodology builds on the historical and contemporary precedents set by Ian McHarg and Richard Forman to establish a strategy for reweaving the natural fluxes in Haidian District, northwestern Beijing. Exploring the site as an accumulation of information at different scales and different times, the research proposes a diachronic look into the natural and cultural history of the site to envision a perspective towards the future.

The execution of the proposal consists of a staged removal of built space. Part of which is destined to the creation of higher-density areas, while the remainder is relocated for the reconnection and articulation of natural networks. The plan acknowledges the cultural developments on site by capitalizing on existing infrastructure for the relocation of the new urban spaces while respecting the historical character of some of the constructions that are preserved as part of the scheme.

链接式发展

人作为整个物种群落的一部分

作为中国的政治中心，北京的城市发展历史给地理景观留下了不可磨灭的痕迹。从前，北京是一个由森林、灌木、草场和湿地包围的丰饶山谷，但是从20世纪初开始的快速城镇化进程割断了人与自然的历史联系。"链接式发展"试图为城市和农业的无计划扩张问题提供一个区域化的解决方案。此方案提出将发展和生产活动高度集中在数个节点区域，使当地的自然系统和生态服务得以恢复，并成为一个新型可持续城市的主要基础设施。

"链接式发展"提出的框架把人类作为一个广阔得多的物种群里的一个成员。方案的分析方法从伊恩·麦克哈格（Ian McHarg）和理查德·福曼（Richard Forman）建立的历史和当代范例上吸取经验，旨在为北京西北部的海淀区建立一个恢复自然联系的策略。本研究方案能够对该区域的自然和文化历史进行历时研究，把这个区域作为信息汇集的中心，通过收集和研究不同尺度、不同时期的信息，构建出未来的发展愿景。

实施这个方案需要对建筑空间进行分步移除。空出的空间一部分用来创造新的高密度区域，另一部分会迁移到其他位置，为重新建立自然生态网络创造条件。方案重视当地的文化发展，因此利用已有的基础设施来吸纳新城市发展需要的空间，同时尊重当地部分建筑的历史特性，予以保护。

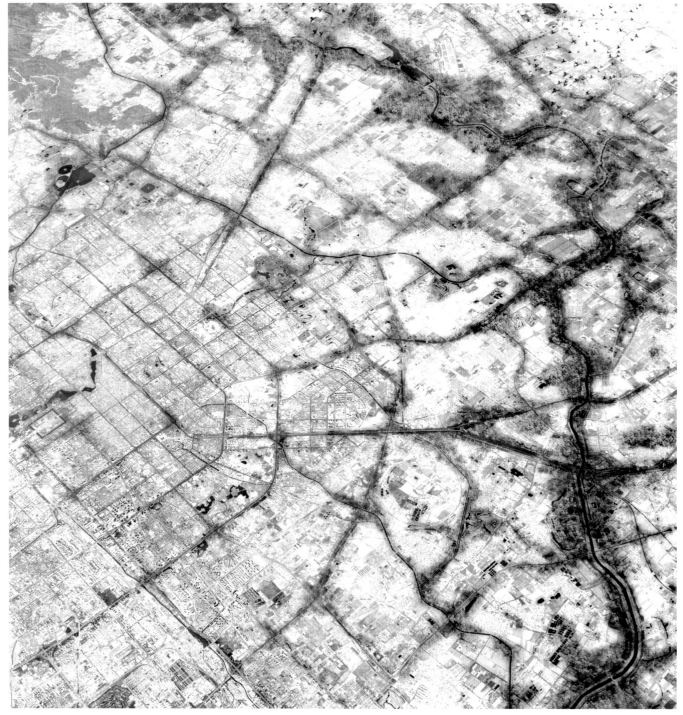

BEIJING VISION
The proposal builds upon existing infrastructure. The city becomes articulated through constructed and natural corridors, These series of Greenbelts and Axes conform a structure similar to a spiderweb that allows for nature to communicate trough the region.
北京远景
本提案基于现有的基础设施，通过建设网络状的自然生态廊道，提高城市中的生态栖息地，平衡自然与城市的发展。

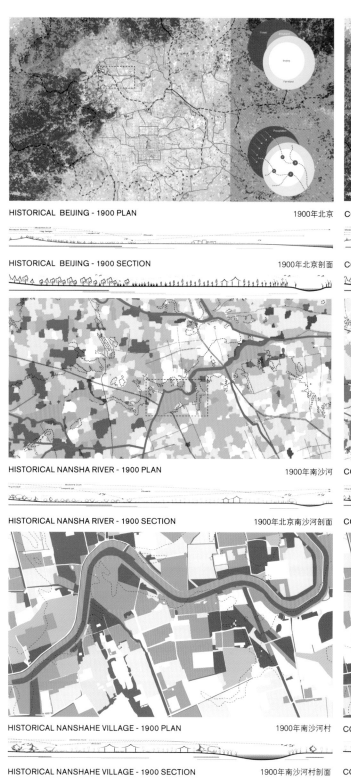

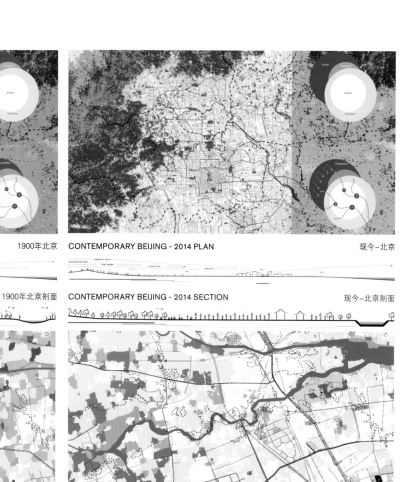

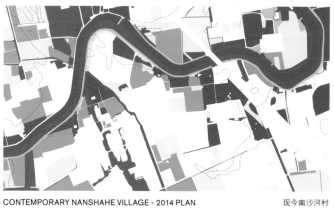

HISTORICAL BEIJING - 1900 PLAN

1900年北京

CONTEMPORARY BEIJING - 2014 PLAN

现今－北京

HISTORICAL BEIJING - 1900 SECTION

1900年北京剖面

CONTEMPORARY BEIJING - 2014 SECTION

现今－北京剖面

HISTORICAL NANSHA RIVER - 1900 PLAN

1900年南沙河

CONTEMPORARY NANSHA RIVER - 2014 PLAN

现今南沙河

HISTORICAL NANSHA RIVER - 1900 SECTION

1900年北京南沙河剖面

CONTEMPORARY NANSHA RIVER - 2014 SECTION

现今南沙河剖面

HISTORICAL NANSHAHE VILLAGE - 1900 PLAN

1900年南沙河村

CONTEMPORARY NANSHAHE VILLAGE - 2014 PLAN

现今南沙河村

HISTORICAL NANSHAHE VILLAGE - 1900 SECTION

1900年南沙河村剖面

CONTEMPORARY NANSHAHE VILLAGE - 2014 SECTION

现今南沙河村剖面

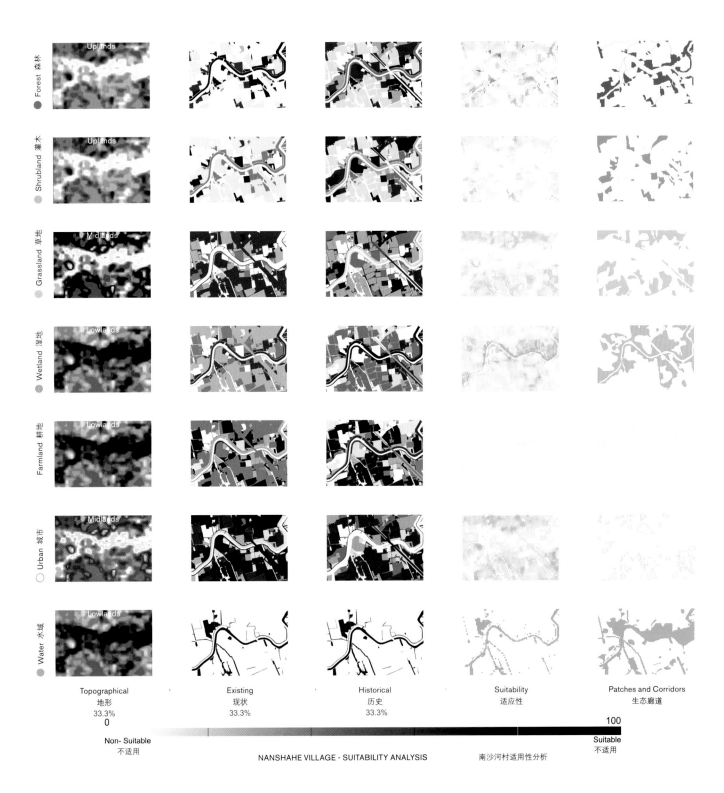

Forest 森林

Shrubland 灌木

Grassland 草地

Wetland 湿地

Farmland 耕地

Urban 城市

Water 水域

Topographical 地形 33.3%	Existing 现状 33.3%	Historical 历史 33.3%	Suitability 适应性	Patches and Corridors 生态廊道

0

Non- Suitable
不适用

100

Suitable
不适用

NANSHAHE VILLAGE - SUITABILITY ANALYSIS   南沙河村适用性分析

NANSHA RIVER VISION

At the river scale, the proposal accomodates a variety of lifestyles and opportunities. By concentrating the population in highly dense nodes, the liberated ground can be employed to reconnect natural systems and reestablish ecosystem services.

南沙河远景

在南沙河范围内，本提案融合多样的生活方式和发展机遇。通过提高建筑密度而释放出的土地将被利用于生态系统的修复和生态基础设施的建设。

NANSHAHE VILLAGE VISION
Edge conditions are embraced throughout the project, challenging contemporary paradigms of human-nature relationships.
南沙河村远景
边界作为提案中重点部分设计，重新思考人与自然的关系

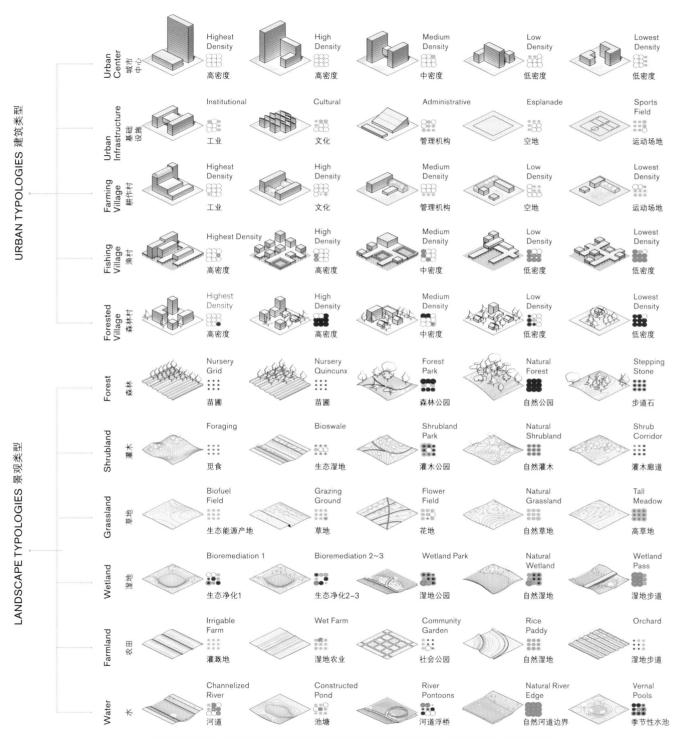

URBAN TYPOLOGIES 建筑类型

Urban Center 城市中心
- Highest Density 高密度
- High Density 高密度
- Medium Density 中密度
- Low Density 低密度
- Lowest Density 低密度

Urban Infrastructure 基础设施
- Institutional 工业
- Cultural 文化
- Administrative 管理机构
- Esplanade 空地
- Sports Field 运动场地

Farming Village 耕作村
- Highest Density 工业
- High Density 文化
- Medium Density 管理机构
- Low Density 空地
- Lowest Density 运动场地

Fishing Village 渔村
- Highest Density 高密度
- High Density 高密度
- Medium Density 中密度
- Low Density 低密度
- Lowest Density 低密度

Forested Village 森林村
- Highest Density 高密度
- High Density 高密度
- Medium Density 中密度
- Low Density 低密度
- Lowest Density 低密度

LANDSCAPE TYPOLOGIES 景观类型

Forest 森林
- Nursery Grid 苗圃
- Nursery Quincunx 苗圃
- Forest Park 森林公园
- Natural Forest 自然公园
- Stepping Stone 步道石

Shrubland 灌木
- Foraging 觅食
- Bioswale 生态湿地
- Shrubland Park 灌木公园
- Natural Shrubland 自然灌木
- Shrub Corridor 灌木廊道

Grassland 草地
- Biofuel Field 生态能源产地
- Grazing Ground 草地
- Flower Field 花地
- Natural Grassland 自然草地
- Tall Meadow 高草地

Wetland 湿地
- Bioremediation 1 生态净化1
- Bioremediation 2~3 生态净化2~3
- Wetland Park 湿地公园
- Natural Wetland 自然湿地
- Wetland Pass 湿地步道

Farmland 农田
- Irrigable Farm 灌溉地
- Wet Farm 湿地农业
- Community Garden 社会公园
- Rice Paddy 自然湿地
- Orchard 湿地步道

Water 水
- Channelized River 河道
- Constructed Pond 池塘
- River Pontoons 河道浮桥
- Natural River Edge 自然河道边界
- Vernal Pools 季节性水池

NANSHAHE VILLAGE STRATEGIES - URBAN AND LANDSCAPE CATALOGUE 南沙河村策略–城市及景观类型

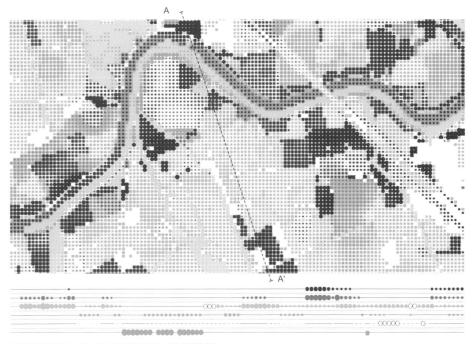

NANSHAHE VILLAGE - SUITABILITY MAP AND SECTION
南沙河村–可持续发展蓝图及剖面

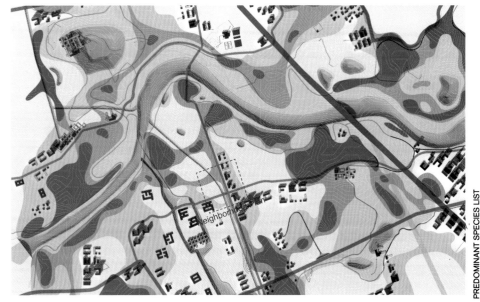

NANSHAHE VILLAGE - PROPOSED PLAN
南沙河村–区域策略

	Species		
Forest	*Koelreuteria Paniculata*, Golden Rain Tree	栾树	
	Acer Truncatum, Shahtung Maple	元宝枫	
	Quercus liaotungensis, Liaodang Oak	辽东栎	
	Quercus Dentata, Daimyo Oak	槲斗树	
	Ulmus Pumila, Siberian Elm	榆树	
	Quercus Variabilis, Chinese Cork Oak	栓皮栎	
	Pinus Tabuliformis, Chinese Red pine	油松	
	Juniperus Chinensis, Chinese Juniper	圆柏	
Shrubland	*Caragana Arborescens*, Siberian Peashrub	树锦鸡儿	
	Cotinus Coggyria, Eurasian Smoketree	黄栌	
	Vitex Negundo var Heterophyllia,	黄荆	
	Spiraea Dasyantha, Spiraea	绒毛绣线菊	
	Deutzia Thunb, Deutzia	溲疏	
	Prunus Davidiana, Wild Peach	山桃	
Grassland	*Orychophragmus Violaceus*	二月兰	
	Viola Philipicca, Chinese Violet	紫花地丁	
	Setaria Viridis, Green Foxtail	狗尾草	
	Lespedeza, Lespedeza	胡枝子	
	Themeda Japonica, Japanese Themeda	黄背草	
	Polygonum Orientale, Oriental Persicary	红蓼	
	Taraxacum Officinale, Common Dandelion	西洋蒲公英	
Wetland	*Nymphoides Peltatum*, Floating Heart	荇菜	
	Nelumbo Nucifera, Indian Lotus	荷花	
	Salix Matsudana, Chinese Willow	柳树	
	Acorus Calamus Linn, Sweet Flag	菖蒲	
	Lythrum Salicaria, Purple Loosestrife	千屈菜	
Farmland	*Corylos Spp*, Hazelnut	榛子	
	Prunus Armeniaca, Apricot	杏	
	Prunus Salicina, Chinese Plum	李子	
	Hydrangea Bretshneideri,	东陵绣球花	
	Lonicera Spp, Honeysuckle	金银花	
	Zea Mays, Indian Corn	玉米	
	Malus Pumila, Apple	苹果	
	Triticum Aestivum, Common Wheat	小麦	
	Oryza Sativa, Rice	水稻	
Urban	*Populus Tomentosa*	毛白杨	
	Populus Davidiana, Aspen	山杨	
	Vaccaria Segetalis, Cow Sapwart	王不留行	
	Ambrosia Trifida, Giant Ragweed	三裂叶豚草	
	Euphorbia Dentata, Toothed Spurge	齿裂大戟	
	Digitaria Chrysoblephara, Crab Digitaria	毛马唐	
	Echinochba Crusgallii, Barnyard Glass	稗子	
	Chenopodian Acuminatum,	尖头叶藜	
	Humus Scadens, Japanese Hop	日本蛇麻草	
	Lagopsis Supine, Common Lagopsis	夏至草	
	Sophora Japonica, Japanese Pagoda Tree	槐树	
	Ailanthus Altissima, Tree of Heaven	臭椿	

PREDOMINANT SPECIES LIST

TERRESTRIAL SYSTEMS AND CONNECTIONS
地形及连接系统

AQUATIC SYSTEMS AND CONNECTIONS
水体及连接系统

CONSTRUCTED SYSTEMS AND CONNECTIONS
建筑及连接系统

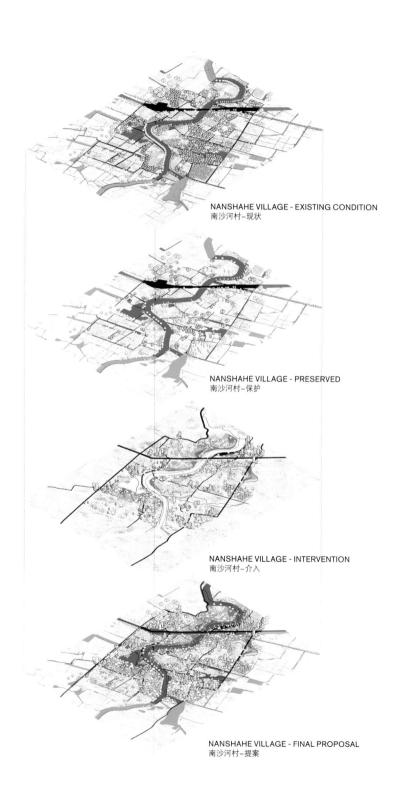

NANSHAHE VILLAGE - EXISTING CONDITION
南沙河村–现状

NANSHAHE VILLAGE - PRESERVED
南沙河村–保护

NANSHAHE VILLAGE - INTERVENTION
南沙河村–介入

NANSHAHE VILLAGE - FINAL PROPOSAL
南沙河村–提案

53

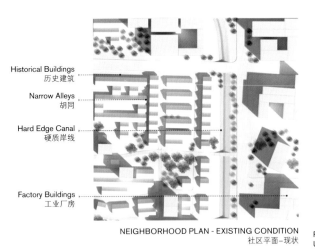

Historical Buildings
历史建筑

Narrow Alleys
胡同

Hard Edge Canal
硬质岸线

Factory Buildings
工业厂房

NEIGHBORHOOD PLAN - EXISTING CONDITION
社区平面–现状

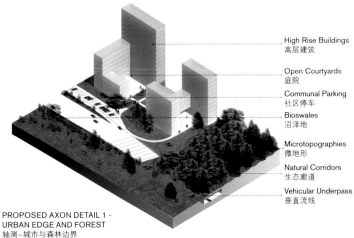

High Rise Buildings
高层建筑

Open Courtyards
庭院

Communal Parking
社区停车

Bioswales
沼泽地

Microtopographies
微地形

Natural Corridors
生态廊道

Vehicular Underpass
垂直流线

PROPOSED AXON DETAIL 1 -
URBAN EDGE AND FOREST
轴测–城市与森林边界

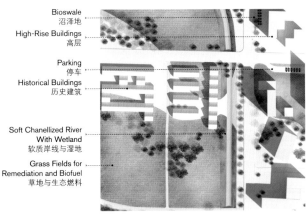

Bioswale
沼泽地

High-Rise Buildings
高层

Parking
停车

Historical Buildings
历史建筑

Soft Chanellized River
With Wetland
软质岸线与湿地

Grass Fields for
Remediation and Biofuel
草地与生态燃料

NEIGHBORHOOD PLAN - PHASE 1 - 1 TO 5 YEARS
社区规划–第一期–1~5年

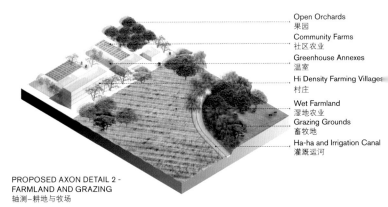

Open Orchards
果园

Community Farms
社区农业

Greenhouse Annexes
温室

Hi Density Farming Villages
村庄

Wet Farmland
湿地农业

Grazing Grounds
畜牧地

Ha-ha and Irrigation Canal
灌溉运河

PROPOSED AXON DETAIL 2 -
FARMLAND AND GRAZING
轴测–耕地与牧场

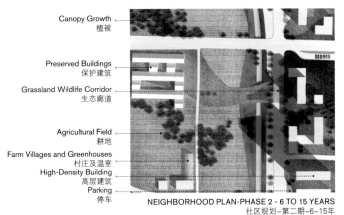

Canopy Growth
植被

Preserved Buildings
保护建筑

Grassland Wildlife Corridor
生态廊道

Agricultural Field
耕地

Farm Villages and Greenhouses
村庄及温室

High-Density Building
高层建筑

Parking
停车

NEIGHBORHOOD PLAN-PHASE 2 - 6 TO 15 YEARS
社区规划–第二期–6~15年

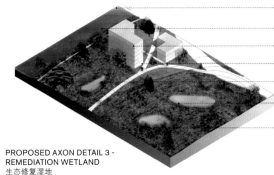

Natural River Edge
自然河岸

Recreational Trails
休闲活动岸线

Medium Rise Buildings
多层建筑

Bike Paths
自行车道

Remediation Pond Phase 2
生态修复水塘–阶段2

Sediment Settling Basin
生态修复洼地

Remediation Pond Phase 1
生态修复水塘–阶段1

PROPOSED AXON DETAIL 3 -
REMEDIATION WETLAND
生态修复湿地

SMART FOOD COMMUNE

Exchanging food – growing knowledge

Omar Davis
Susan Nguyen

Nansha River's ecological system is broken and systemic change is tied to two major interventions. The first intervention reconfigures the current agricultural landscape and the second decreases the growing gap in knowledge between the local and regional community to prevent continuous system failure. Knowledge of the system, knowledge of a more sustainable way, knowledge of one's impact to the system, and knowledge of how to advance the system to fit the modern periurban, urban, and rural space. We propose because of Nansha River's common ecological challenge and unique location in the Beijing, it is the ideal experimental lab space for the investigation of agriculture and knowledge as tools to fix the broken nutrient flux for the region.

THREE MAIN GUIDING PRINCIPLES:

1. The ratio of farmland to people makes local food security unrealistic, but the interventions still attempt to maximize the agricultural product in a balanced system through reconfiguring the land.

2. In developing the interventions, priority was given to the existing context, particularly residences and social nodes.

3. Food in Chinese culture is as much a nutrient as it is a social glue. From the round dining table to large banquet halls, the buying, selling, preparing, serving, and eating of food are integral in the social dynamics of the Chinese community. As we think of agriculture and the changes of these social moments and the spaces they occupy, we want to preserve their essence in our proposal.

智能食物社区

食物交换–知识增长

南沙河的生态系统被破坏，我们主要通过两个主要人为干预来实现系统上的改变。第一个是重新构建农业景观，第二个是缩小地方和区域的社会群体在对一些问题认识上的差距，防止系统继续被破坏。这包括对系统的认识、对可持续的认识、对个体对系统的影响的认识以及对系统如何适应现代郊区、城市和乡村空间发展的认识。南沙河具有的普遍生态挑战以及其独特的地理位置使其可以作为一个理想的实验场所，来探讨如何利用农业和知识作为工具来修复该区域被破坏的营养流。

三个主要的指导原则：

1. 目前的人均耕地比使得保障本地粮食安全不太现实，但我们将尝试不破坏生态系统的平衡，而是利用重新构建土地的方式来最大化粮食产量。

2. 在干预方案中，当地现有的环境会受到优先保护，尤其是居住区和社会节点。

3. 食物在中国文化中既是营养的来源，也是社会的黏结剂。从圆餐桌到大宴会厅，食物的采购、销售、准备、上菜以及食用都是中国社会动态的一部分。考虑到农业和与之相关的社会发展的变化以及农业用地空间的意义和重要性，我们将在方案中保留并体现这些要素。

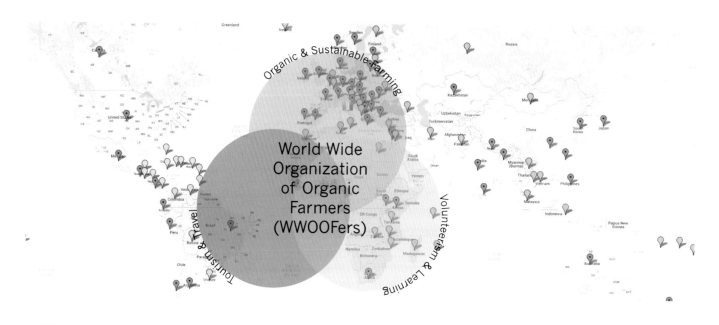

World Wide
Organization
of Organic
Farmers
(WWOOFers)

Organic & Sustainable Farming

Volunteerism & Learning

Tourism & Travel

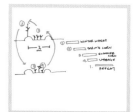
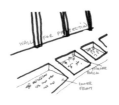
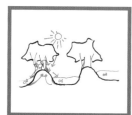

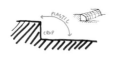
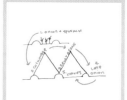
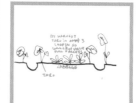

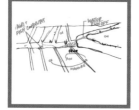

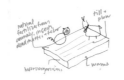

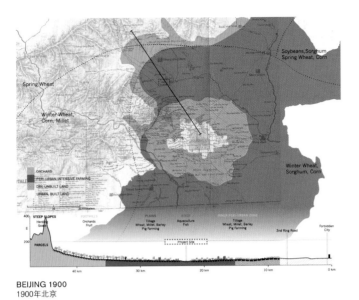

BEIJING 1900
1900年北京

BEIJING 2010
2010年北京

NANSHAHE 1900

NANSHAHE 2010

NANSHA River 1900
1900年南沙河

NANSHA River 2010
2010年南沙河

DAY

WEEK

SEASON

Local
本地

Metro
城市

Domestic
区域

International
国际

1
FISH PONDS
鱼塘

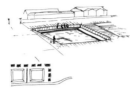

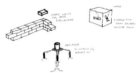

4
IRRIGATION
灌溉

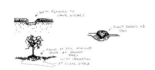

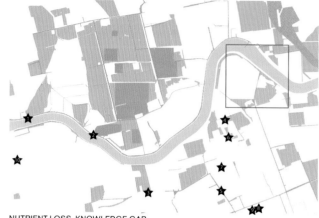

NUTRIENT LOSS, KNOWLEDGE GAP
营养流失，知识获取

2
GREENHOUSES
温室

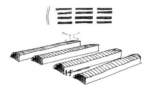

5
IN/ORGANIC WASTE
有机废料

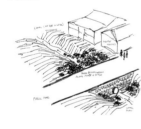

7
INFORMAL MARKET
临时市场

9
PACKAGED GOODS MARKET
批发市场

3
MONO FORESTS
单一树种森林

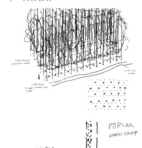

6
HUMAN WASTE
人畜废料

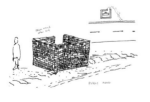

8
FORMAL MARKET
社区市场

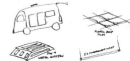

10
FOOD CORRIDOR
食品街

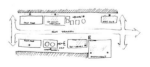

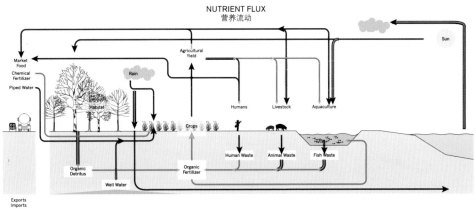

NUTRIENT FLUX
营养流动

Sun

Market
Food
Chemical
Fertilizer
Piped Water

Agricultural
Yield

Rain

Habitat

Humans

Livestock

Aquaculture

Crops

Organic
Detritus

Well Water

Organic
Fertilizer

Human Waste

Animal Waste

Fish Waste

Exports
Imports

KNOWLEDGE FLUX
营养流动

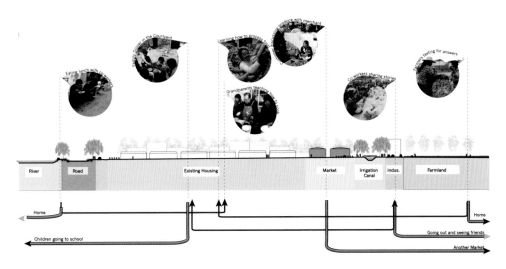

COMPOSITION OF NANSHA River
南沙河构成

River   Road   Existing Housing   Market   Irrigation Canal   indus.   Farmland

Home   Home

Children going to school   Going out and seeing friends

Another Market

DAY

WEEK

SEASON

Local
本地

Metro
城市

Domestic
区域

International
国际

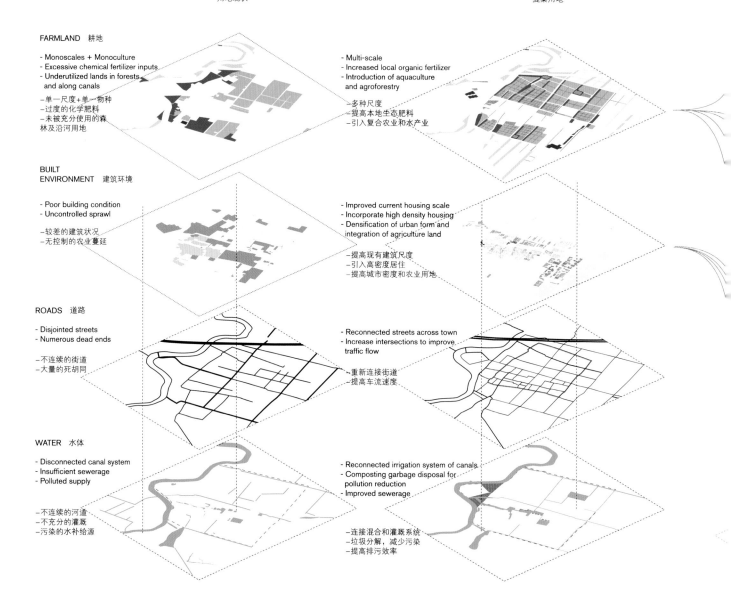

FARMLAND 耕地

- Monoscales + Monoculture
- Excessive chemical fertilizer inputs
- Underutilized lands in forests
  and along canals

－单一尺度＋单一物种
－过度的化学肥料
－未被充分使用的森
  林及沿河用地

- Multi-scale
- Increased local organic fertilizer
- Introduction of aquaculture
  and agroforestry

－多种尺度
－提高本地生态肥料
－引入复合农业和水产业

BUILT
ENVIRONMENT 建筑环境

- Poor building condition
- Uncontrolled sprawl

－较差的建筑状况
－无控制的农业蔓延

- Improved current housing scale
- Incorporate high density housing
- Densification of urban form and
  integration of agriculture land

－提高现有建筑尺度
－引入高密度居住
－提高城市密度和农业用地

ROADS 道路

- Disjointed streets
- Numerous dead ends

－不连续的街道
－大量的死胡同

- Reconnected streets across town
- Increase intersections to improve
  traffic flow

－重新连接街道
－提高车流速度

WATER 水体

- Disconnected canal system
- Insufficient sewerage
- Polluted supply

－不连续的河道
－不充分的灌溉
－污染的水补给源

- Reconnected irrigation system of canals
- Composting garbage disposal for
  pollution reduction
- Improved sewerage

－连接混合和灌溉系统
－垃圾分解，减少污染
－提高排污效率

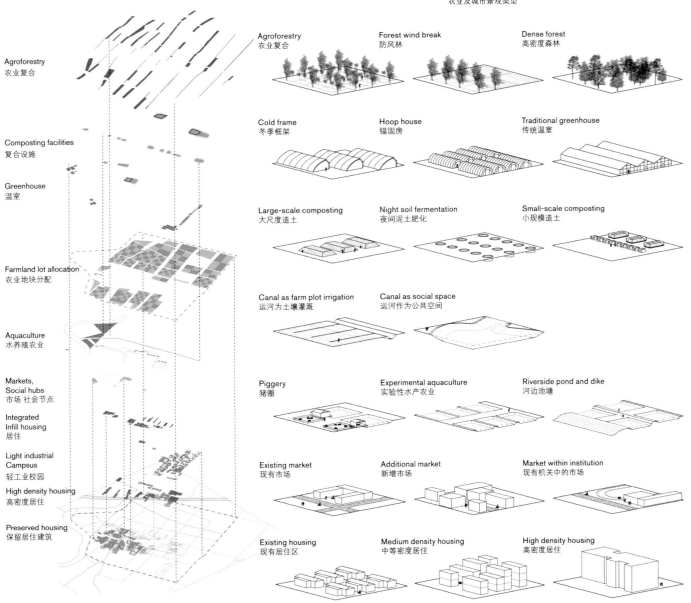

Agroforestry
农业复合

Composting facilities
复合设施

Greenhouse
温室

Farmland lot allocation
农业地块分配

Aquaculture
水养殖农业

Markets,
Social hubs
市场 社会节点

Integrated
Infill housing
居住

Light industrial
Campsus
轻工业校园

High density housing
高密度居住

Preserved housing
保留居住建筑

AGRICULTURAL AND URBAN LANDSCAPE TOOLKIT
农业及城市景观类型

Agroforestry
农业复合

Forest wind break
防风林

Dense forest
高密度森林

Cold frame
冬季框架

Hoop house
锚固房

Traditional greenhouse
传统温室

Large-scale composting
大尺度造土

Night soil fermentation
夜间泥土肥化

Small-scale composting
小规模造土

Canal as farm plot irrigation
运河为土壤灌溉

Canal as social space
运河作为公共空间

Piggery
猪圈

Experimental aquaculture
实验性水产农业

Riverside pond and dike
河边池塘

Existing market
现有市场

Additional market
新增市场

Market within institution
现有机关中的市场

Existing housing
现有居住区

Medium density housing
中等密度居住

High density housing
高密度居住

NANSHAHE VILLAGE COLLABORATIVE FARMS AND MARKETPLACE, 2030
南沙河村农业及农产品市场远景，2030

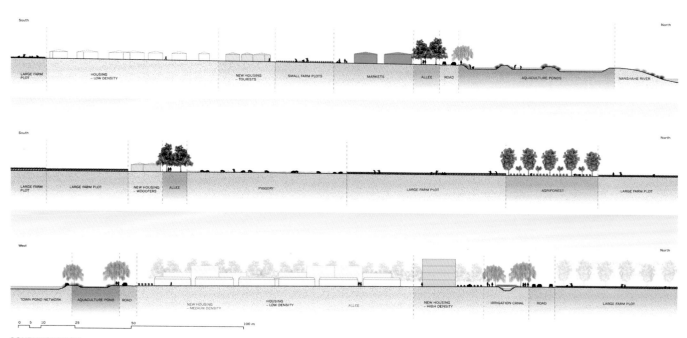

SCHEME SECTION
区域剖面

PUBLIC FOOD MARKETS
EXISTING HOUSING – LOW DENSITY
NEW HOUSING – MEDIUM DENSITY
NEW HOUSING – HIGH DENSITY
LIGHT INDUSTRIAL
AGROFORESTS
CROPLAND
LIVESTOCK PASTURES
GREENHOUSES
COMPOST/FERTILIZER FACILITIES
AQUACULTURE & POND/DIKE SYSTEMS
CANALS, PONDS & WATERWAYS

0   250   500   1000 m

SITE PLAN
基地平面图

FROM BLACK TO GREEN

From monomania of coal to thermodynamic depth

Zander Hannes

Erin Hannes

This project works to shift the paradigm in Beijing, from a single mindset of energy as something to be consumed to a larger view of the ecological, cultural, and economic energetics of landscape. Only by understanding this excess of energy that exists within the landscape can we think radically about Beijing's development and how to reconnect large scale systems. Starting with the existing landscape media, we approach the site through negative planning. Ecological infrastructure serves as the organizing system for the design of urban space.

Using a layered and rich forestry approach, unlike the current monocultural plantations on the periphery of Beijing, we propose a productive greenbelt where a unique landscape experience is created, local business and biodiversity are stimulated, and existing infrastructure is used efficiently. With the forest as the main driver of our greenbelt, we are setting up a method of planning at a range of scales, from local microclimates to Beijing's anthropogenic biome. This diversified forest creates a new place of recreational experience for the people of Beijing. It also creates opportunities for local villages such as the production of biofuel. The removal of concrete channels and creation of wetlands along the Nansha River creates a resilient ecological infrastructure, driving the creation of green fingers that interweave village and forest. Along this park spine, local economies are activated such as waste recycling, soil production, and carpentry. These cultural hubs change the current condition from remote societies to local communities attached to their environs.

由黑至绿

从单一的煤炭能源消费到热力多样性能源

这个提案目的在于以北京为例，转变人们对能源的固有观念，它不单纯是一种消耗品，而且可以是流动在景观中的生态、文化和经济能量。只有看到了这部分潜在的能源才能从根本上思考北京未来的发展以及如何重塑大尺度系统之间的联系。以现在的景观作为试探，我们对其进行"反规划"的实践，即在城市空间设计中以生态基础设施作为首要组织系统。

摒弃北京城环状栽植单一种类的树木的做法，我们建议构建由多层次、种类丰富的森林式植被群组成的具有生产效益的绿带。这不仅创造出了独特的景观，刺激当地经济的发展和生物多样性的恢复，也能促进当地基础设施的高效利用。以森林作为绿带的功能主体，我们的设计方法能够适用于各种尺度，从本地区的微气候到整个北京的人为生物群落。多样化的森林环境为北京人民提供了休闲新去处，还为当地村民提供了生产生物燃料的机会。移除混凝土河道和重建湿地系统为南沙河营造了具有适应力的生态基础设施，也有利于村落和森林间天然绿带的形成。以公园为支撑点，本地经济产业，如废物回收利用，土壤再造和木工产业都能被激活，这种文化中心也把原本边缘的社会群体改造成与周围环境紧密相连的本地社群。

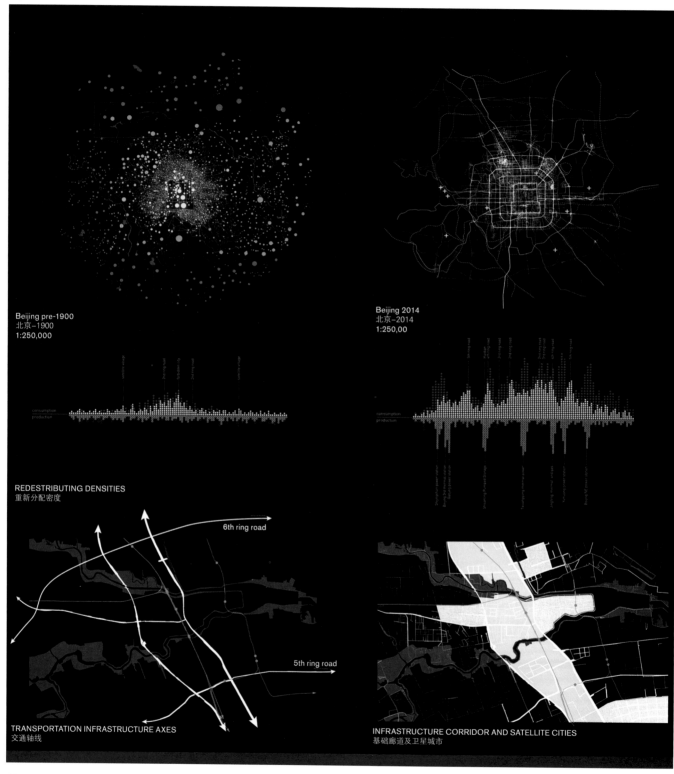

Beijing pre-1900
北京-1900
1:250,000

Beijing 2014
北京-2014
1:250,00

REDISTRIBUTING DENSITIES
重新分配密度

6th ring road

5th ring road

TRANSPORTATION INFRASTRUCTURE AXES
交通轴线

INFRASTRUCTURE CORRIDOR AND SATELLITE CITIES
基础廊道及卫星城市

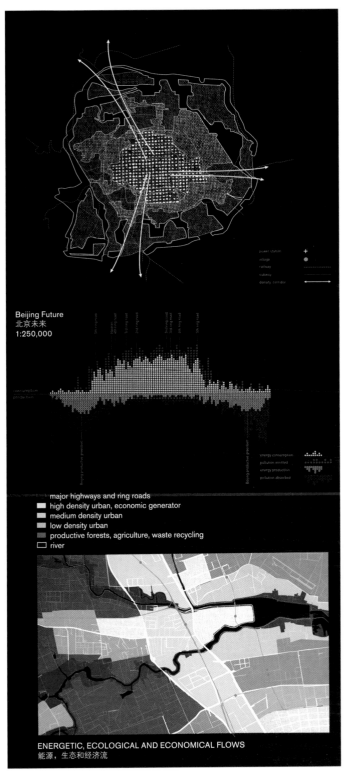

Beijing Future
北京未来
1:250,000

major highways and ring roads
high density urban, economic generator
medium density urban
low density urban
productive forests, agriculture, waste recycling
river

ENERGETIC, ECOLOGICAL AND ECONOMICAL FLOWS
能源，生态和经济流

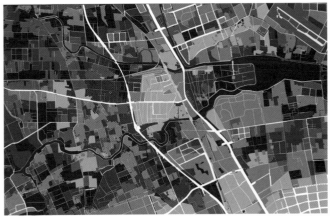

2014: DENSITIES OF ENERGY CONSUMPTION
2014年密度及能源消耗

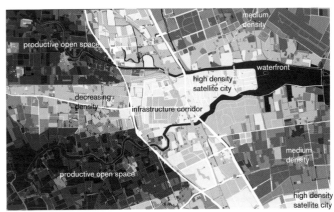

FUTURE: REDISTRIBUTED DENSITIES
未来：重新分配密度

– – subway   — train   energy consumption   infrastructure motorized transportation   low density housing
high rise, intensive industry   intensive agriculture, active brownfield, construction
high density, extensive industry, transfer sites   extensive open space, water

SECTION AA'
剖面AA'

SECTION BB'
剖面BB'

SECTION CC'
剖面CC'

69

BEFORE: COAL
现状：煤炭能源

AFTER: BIOMASS ENERGY
提案：生态能源

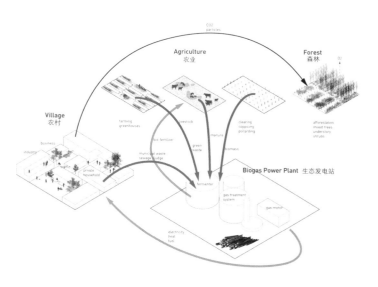

ECONOMY
经济

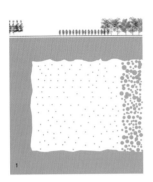

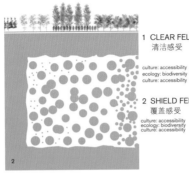

1 CLEAR FELLING
清洁感受

culture: accessibility
ecology: biodiversity
culture: accessibility

2 SHIELD FELLING
覆盖感受

culture: accessibility
ecology: biodiversity
culture: accessibility

1 WATER SYSTEM
水系统

3 FORESTATION
造林

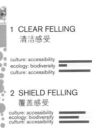

2 TRANSPORTATION
交通系统

4 CULTURAL PROGRAMS AND
INFRASTRUCTURE
文化产业及基础设施

BIOGAS POWER PLANT AND WOOD PROCESSING
生态燃气发电及木料处理

energy production: electricity
bio-fertilizer production
bio-fuel production
woodchip production
sustainable energy

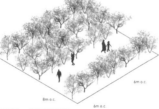

ORCHARD
果园

fruit production
meadow / moving
biodiversity
local food
landscape aesthetic
temporary open space

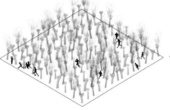

POLLARDING / COPPICING
截枝助长

wood production, biogas
basket caning
landscape aesthetic

COMPOSTING AND SOIL PRODUCTION
堆土造肥

soil production
green waste collecting
local energy production, heat / methane
recycling, waste reduction

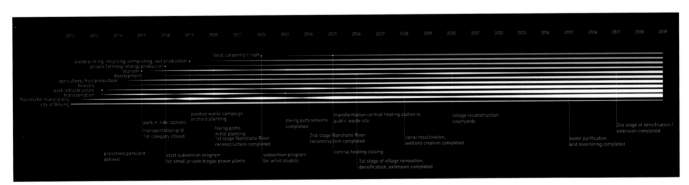

ECONOMIC INFLUENCE OVER TIME
产生经济影响时间线

BEFORE:REMOTE
现状：远程运输

AFTER: LOCAL
提案：本地再生能源

CULTURE
文化

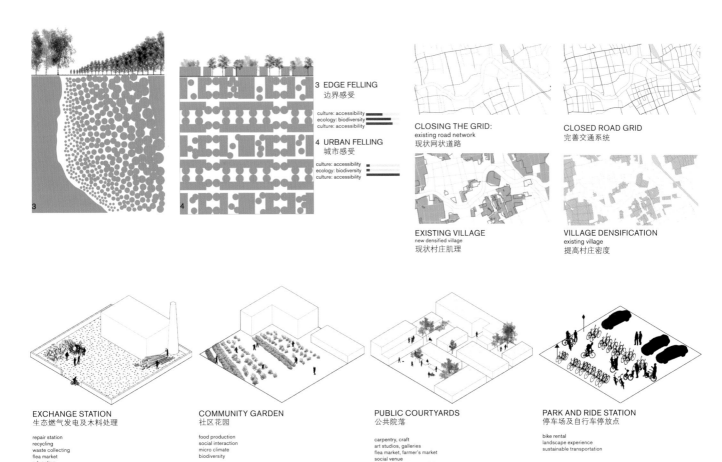

3 EDGE FELLING
   边界感受

culture: accessibility
ecology: biodiversity
culture: accessibility

4 URBAN FELLING
   城市感受

culture: accessibility
ecology: biodiversity
culture: accessibility

CLOSING THE GRID:
existing road network
现状网状道路

CLOSED ROAD GRID
完善交通系统

EXISTING VILLAGE
new densified village
现状村庄肌理

VILLAGE DENSIFICATION
existing village
提高村庄密度

EXCHANGE STATION
生态燃气发电及木料处理

repair station
recycling
waste collecting
flea market
education
art studios, waste art
social interaction and exchange
product recycling and second hand articles

COMMUNITY GARDEN
社区花园

food production
social interaction
micro climate
biodiversity

PUBLIC COURTYARDS
公共院落

carpentry, craft
art studios, galleries
flea market, farmer's market
social venue
pocket park, urban gardening

PARK AND RIDE STATION
停车场及自行车停放点

bike rental
landscape experience
sustainable transportation

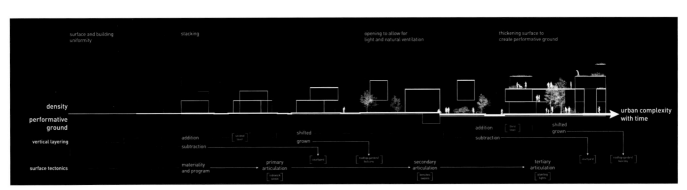

INCREASING SOCIAL DYNAMICS
增加社会多样性

BEFORE:RIGID
现状：固定

AFTER:RESILIENT
提案：灵活

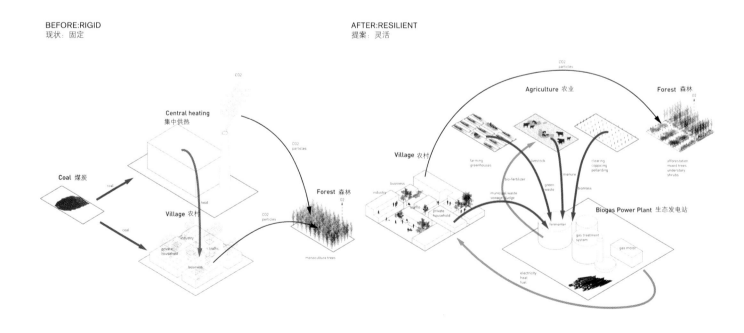

ECOLOGY
生态

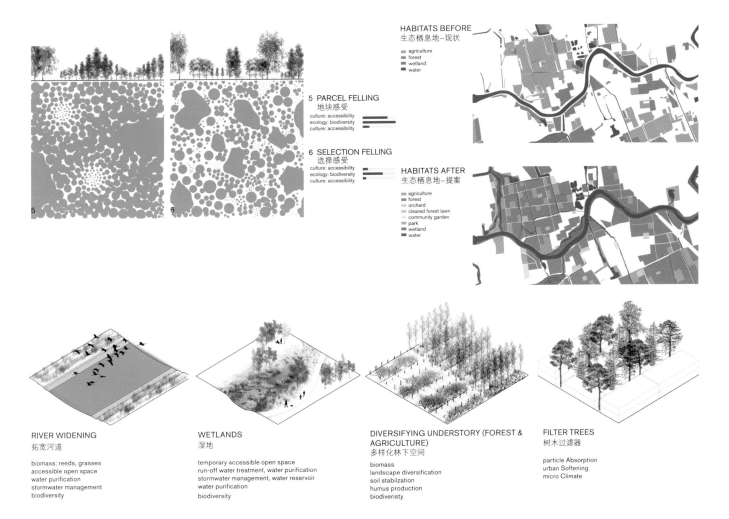

HABITATS BEFORE
生态栖息地－现状
agriculture
forest
wetland
water

5 PARCEL FELLING
地块感受
culture: accessibility
ecology: biodiversity
culture: accessibility

6 SELECTION FELLING
选择感受
culture: accessibility
ecology: biodiversity
culture: accessibility

HABITATS AFTER
生态栖息地－提案
agriculture
forest
orchard
cleared forest lawn
community garden
park
wetland
water

RIVER WIDENING
拓宽河道

biomass: reeds, grasses
accessible open space
water purification
stormwater management
biodiversity

WETLANDS
湿地

temporary accessible open space
run-off water treatment, water purification
stormwater management, water reservoir
water purification
biodiversity

DIVERSIFYING UNDERSTORY (FOREST & AGRICULTURE)
多样化林下空间

biomass
landscape diversification
soil stabilzation
humus production
biodiversity

FILTER TREES
树木过滤器

particle Absorption
urban Softening
micro Climate

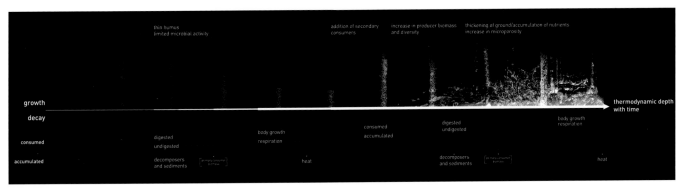

thin humus
limited microbial activity

addition of secondary consumers

increase in producer biomass and diversity

thickening of ground/accumulation of nutrients
increase in microporosity

growth

thermodynamic depth with time

decay

consumed

body growth
respiration

consumed
accumulated

digested
undigested

body growth
respiration

consumed

digested
undigested

decomposers
and sediments

decomposers
and sediments

accumulated

heat

heat

BIOLOGICAL ENERGETIC ACCUMULATION
生态能源聚集

75

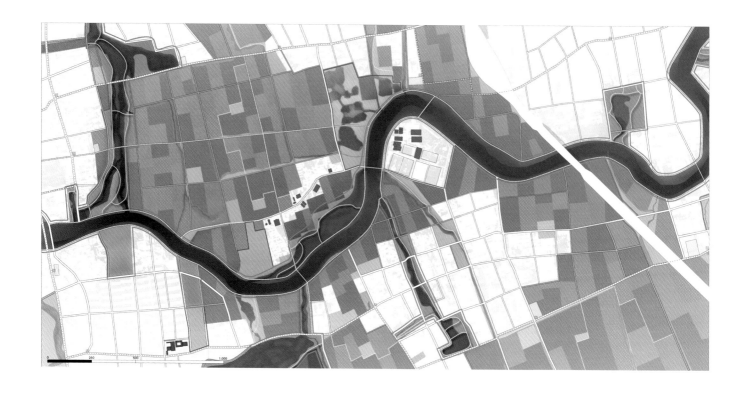

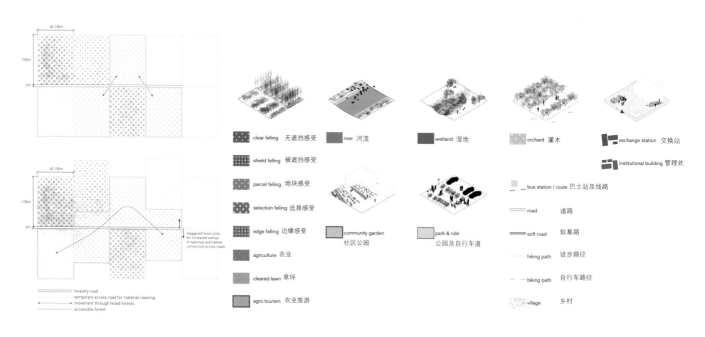

clear felling 无遮挡感受	river 河流	wetland 湿地	orchard 灌木	exchange station 交换站	
shield felling 被遮挡感受				institutional building 管理处	
parcel felling 地块感受				bus station / route 巴士站及线路	
selection felling 选择感受				road 道路	
edge felling 边缘感受	community garden 社区公园	park & ride 公园及自行车道		soft road 软基路	
agriculture 农业				hiking path 徒步路径	
cleared lawn 草坪				biking path 自行车路径	
agro tourism 农业旅游				village 乡村	

forestry road
temporary access road for material clearing
movement through felled forests
accessible forest

40-100m

-100m

6m

staggered forest plots
for increased overlap
of openings and habitat
connectivity across roads

FOREST
森林

RIVER
河流

VILLAGE
村庄

SECTION 1
剖面 1

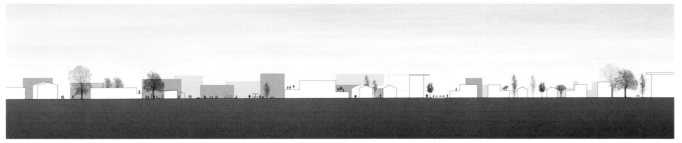

SECTION 2
剖面 2

A LOT
Transforming Beijing's greenbelt

Cynthia Dehlavi
Frank Refuerzo

一个实验场
北京绿带的转型

The New Beijing Green Belt acts as an opportunity to unite three varied people groups (migrant, permanent and visitors) through a productive system of allotment gardens and forest edge buffers. By joining government authority with private ownership, the new beijing green belt has an adaptable framework which is safeguarded from major development. As an escape from the city, a food source, or a place of residence, this new development seeks to freshen the air while uniting the fluxing population.

Our strategy becomes a battle of ownership to optimize maintenance of the new greenbelt. How can we allow for the highest degree of flexibility and freedom, while giving the greenbelt rules for survival? A sequence of edges create a buffer for ecological migration, urban pollution filtration and visual division. The village edge, the water edge and the infrastructural edge are under the control of nearby villages. Abundant character can derive from the divided responsibility.The interstitial space between village, water and infrastructure, within the proposed green belt, becomes available for private ownership. A grid, based on existing infrastructure, creates the framework for parcel and purchase. Parcel sizes vary from 0.25 mu (XS) to 10 mu (XL). A new commune is able to emerge from rules devised for the land.

方案提出由私用园地和森林缓冲带构成具有生产力的新北京绿带，并以此把不同人群（外来移民，北京居民和游客）联系起来。政府与私人合作的方式使此绿带适应当地条件，保护该区域免于卷入快速城镇化的洪流。保持自己的相对独立，生产粮食，适宜居住，这个发展区域将在净化空气的同时也能连接各个人群。

为了最有效地维护这个绿带，我们提出的策略需要解决绿带所有权问题。如何能够做到给予它最大程度的灵活性又为其设定不可或缺的管理规则呢？一系列的边界缓冲带起到方便生态移民，过滤城市污染和视觉隔离的作用。乡村边界、水边界和基础设施边界是由附近的乡村负责管理的。管理责任划分有利于产生各自的特色。在绿带中乡村、水体和基础设施之间的空隙将允许被私人拥有，可以基于现有基础设施的网格系统来建立划分及买卖地块的框架。每个地块的大小从0.25亩到10亩不等。按照这种管理规则，一个新的社区就产生了。

THE GREENBELT-BEIJING TO NANSHA RIVER
城市绿环–北京到南沙河

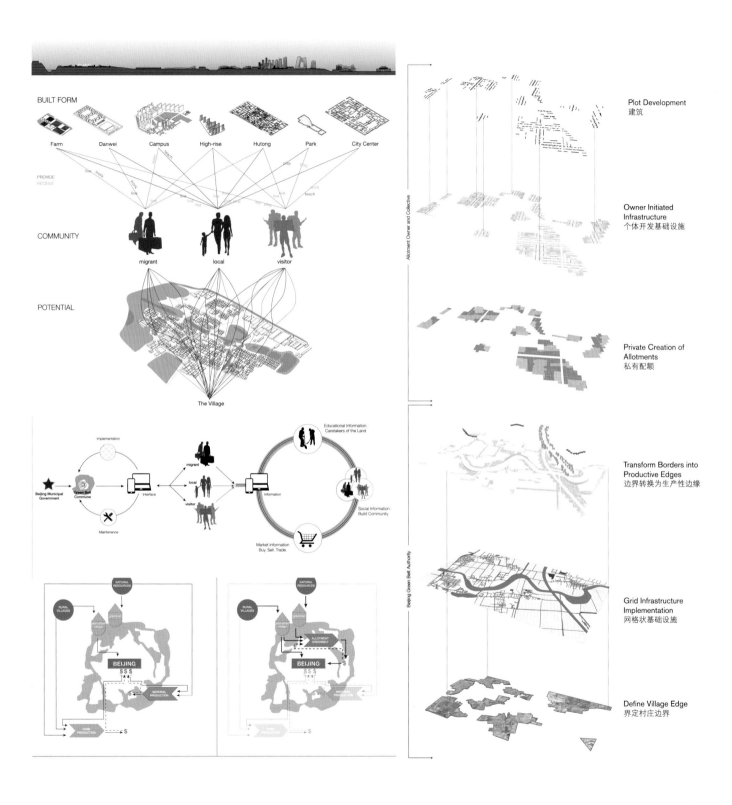

BUILT FORM

Farm Danwei Campus High-rise Hutong Park City Center

PROVIDE
RECEIVE

COMMUNITY

migrant local visitor

POTENTIAL

The Village

Plot Development
建筑

Owner Initiated
Infrastructure
个体开发基础设施

Private Creation of
Allotments
私有配额

Transform Borders into
Productive Edges
边界转换为生产性边缘

Grid Infrastructure
Implementation
网格状基础设施

Define Village Edge
界定村庄边界

81

Pre-1900: TheForbidden City

1958: The Socialist City

1992: The Market-Oriented City

2003: The Green Olympic City to
The "Eco-City"

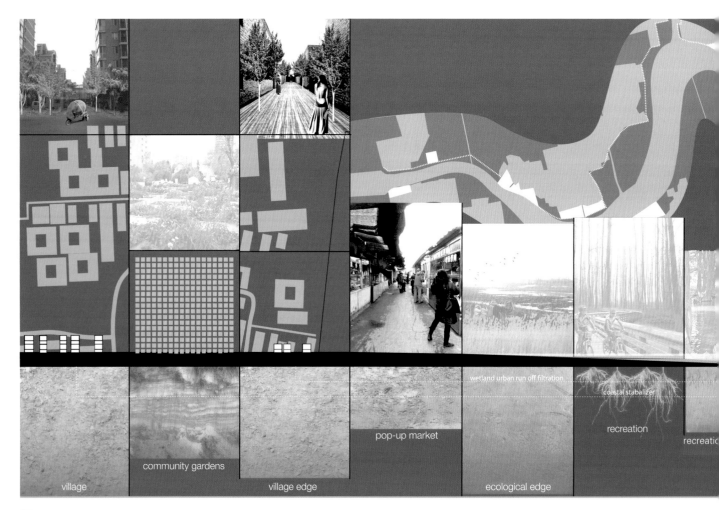

wetland urban run off filtration

coastal stabalizer

pop-up market

recreation

recreatio

community gardens

village

village edge

ecological edge

1935
London Green Belt

1935
Greater Moscow Plan for Reconstruction

1958
The Randstad's Green Heart

1971
Melbourne's Green Wedges

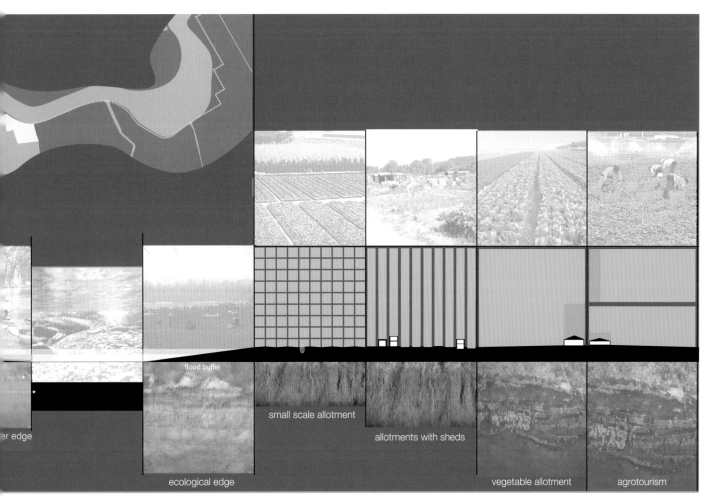

flood buffer

small scale allotment

allotments with sheds

er edge

ecological edge

vegetable allotment

agrotourism

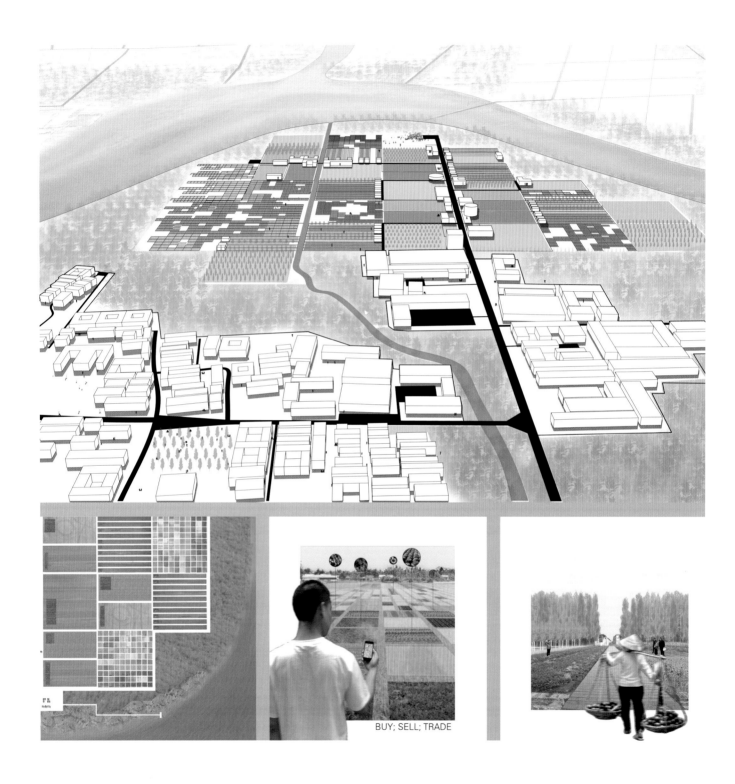

BUY; SELL; TRADE

VILLAGE EDGE
村庄边界

XL–5% at 1 floor
2% at 2 floor

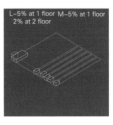

L–5% at 1 floor M–5% at 1 floor
2% at 2 floor

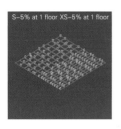

S–5% at 1 floor XS–5% at 1 floor

Government adds to existing infrastructure

First plots develop along major roads

Owners collaborate to build new roads

Finer grained roads for smaller plots

WATER EDGE
水域边界

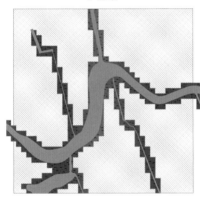

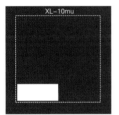

XL–10mu

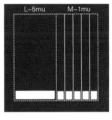

L–5mu　M–1mu

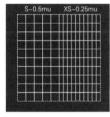

S–0.5mu　XS–0.25mu

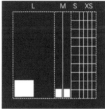

L　M　S　XS

Village Filtration Buffer

Ecological Buffer

Infrastructure Buffer

System–wide Connective Buffers

INFRASTRUCTURAL EDGE
基础设施边界

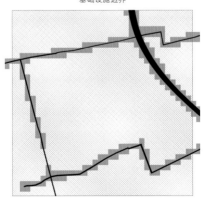

Imperial Grid

Majority Grid

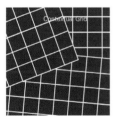

Contextual Grid

Road Implementation Strategy

Village Edge

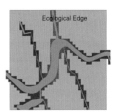

Ecological Edge

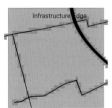

Infrastructure Edge

Interstitial Space Remains

URBAN UNIT COLLAGE

Building a new commune in Beijing

Shanji Li

城市单元拼贴

建设北京新社区

The project is trying to test a new urbanization model by constructing a collage of different urban units in the periphery of Beijing. For the last century, Beijing has gone through different phases of the urban development including agricultural moment featured by Feudalism, industrial moment featured by communist economy and urbanization moment featured by rapid urbanization. Within the last phase, Beijing has accomplished massive urban development but also resulted large monocultural urban blocks and repetitional urban fabrics. The project is located at the edge of the urban sprawl, which provides the opportunity for testing a new development strategy. The project started from a study of analyzing different mega urban blocks along the river in the neighborhood area. Unit composition and structure have been the focus of the study because of the historical context of work unit and also the cultural concept of the unit. The existing urban village, wet land park, office, villa, and apartment units are analyzed in three different scales: urban unit scale, subdivision scale and also cell unit scale. The segmentation, composition and dimension have been studied according to different scales, and matrix and modulization were laid out based on this analysis. The overall matrix is developed from the structural relationship of the landscape infrastructure and the modulization is based on the different cell unit dimensions. From these matrix and modulization, a new commune is developed with a mixture of different surrounding urban units and the landscape infrastructure become the spine of the new commune and also the medium for the interaction of different urban units.

本方案通过在北京市郊建设一个新型混合社区，对一个创新的城市化模型进行实验。从20世纪开始，北京经历了城镇化的不同发展阶段，从封建时代的农业发展，到社会主义的工业时代再到如今的快速城镇化阶段。从目前的发展阶段来看，北京虽然完成了大规模的城镇化，但是建成的街区风格单一，城市形态重复。本项目位于城市扩张的边缘，有利于试验这种新的发展策略。项目首先对沿河两岸的大城市街区开始分块研究。因为历史和文化观念的因素，我们把街区的单元构成以及结构作为研究的重点，对现存的村落、湿地公园、办公楼、别墅和公寓单元分别从三个尺度进行分析：城市单元尺度，细分尺度以及单元尺度，并对每个尺度上呈现的分隔、组合和规模都进行了分析。在这个分析的基础上我们得出了新的结构和单元规划。总体结构是建立在景观基础设施结构上的，而单元规划是基于不同单元的规模。这种规划下的新社区具有混合社区的丰富性和多样性，而景观基础设施既是这个新社区的中脊，又充当着不同城市单元间互动的媒介。

Agricultural Moment [1900/1922] 农业时代(1900/1922)

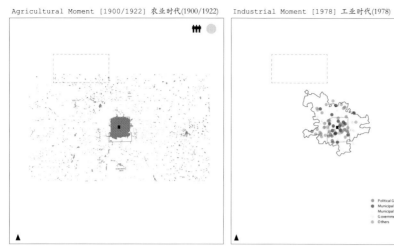

Industrial Moment [1978] 工业时代(1978)

Political Government Institution
Municipal Party Department
Municipal Government Department
Government Business Unit
Others

Urban Moment [2012/2013] 城市化时代(2012/2013)

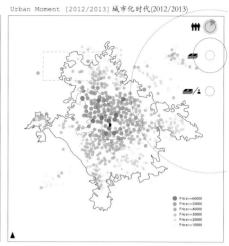

Price>=60000
Price>=50000
Price>=40000
Price>=30000
Price>=20000
Price>=10000

Agricultural Moment [1900/1922] 农业时代(1900/1922)

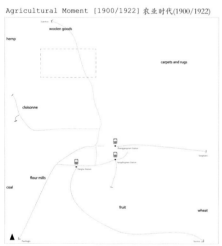

Industrial Moment [1978] 工业时代(1978)

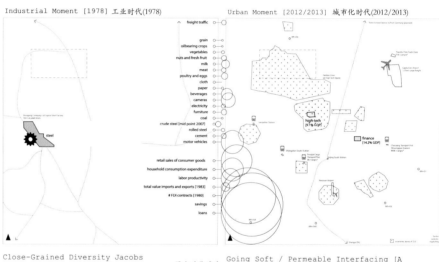

freight traffic
grain
oilbearing crops
vegetables
nuts and fresh fruit
milk
meat
poultry and eggs
cloth
paper
beverages
cameras
electricity
furniture
coal
crude steel [mid point 2007]
rolled steel
cement
motor vehicles

retail sales of consumer goods
household consumption expenditure
labor productivity
total value imports and exports [1983]
FDI contracts [1980]
savings
loans

Urban Moment [2012/2013] 城市化时代(2012/2013)

high-tech
finance

Functional City CIAM [1930s] 功能分区城市（1920s）

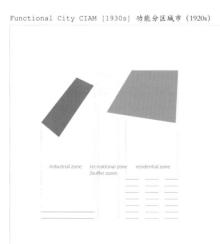

industrial zone   recreational zone   residential zone
                   (buffer zone)

Close-Grained Diversity Jacobs Jacobs / Mumford [1960s]   混合功能城市

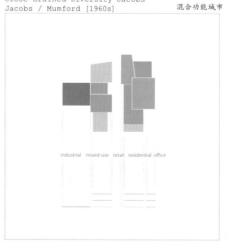

industrial mixed-use retail residential office

Going Soft / Permeable Interfacing [A New Commune] 软化/渗透/交流（新公社）

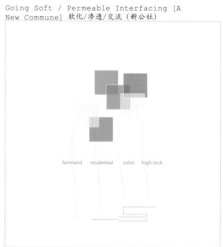

farmland   residential   soho   high-tech

Intervention/Diversification

转化／多样化

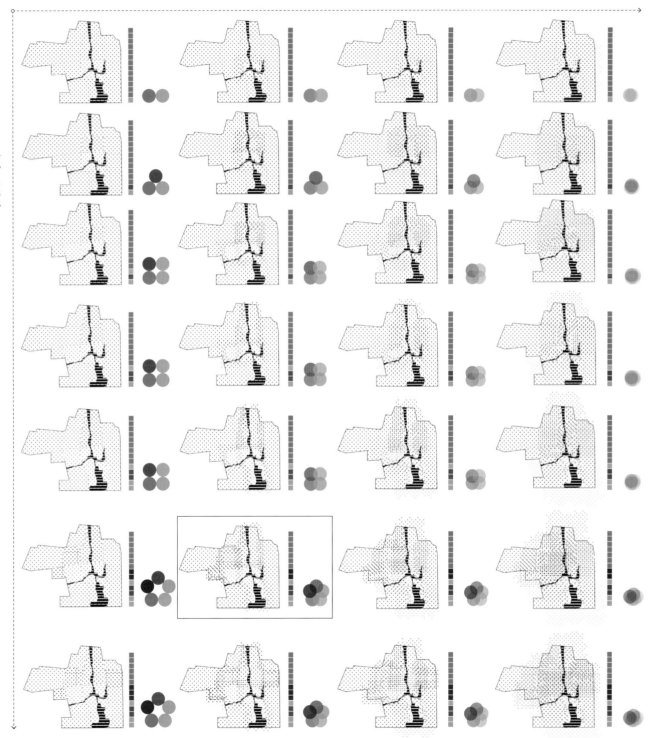

A. URBAN UNIT AND SEGMENT　城市单元及片段

A-1-Wet Land Park-Urban Unit
A-1-湿地-城市单元

A-2-Urban Village-Urban Unit
A-2-城中村-城市单元

A-3-office-Urban Unit
A-3-办公-城市单元

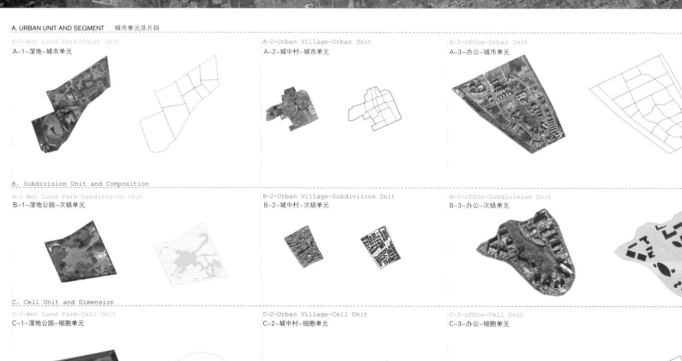

B. Subdivision Unit and Composition

B-1-Wet Land Park-Subdivision Unit
B-1-湿地公园-次级单元

B-2-Urban Village-Subdivision Unit
B-2-城中村-次级单元

B-3-office-Subdivision Unit
B-3-办公-次级单元

C. Cell Unit and Dimension

C-1-Wet Land Park-Cell Unit
C-1-湿地公园-细胞单元

C-2-Urban Village-Cell Unit
C-2-城中村-细胞单元

C-3-office-Cell Unit
C-3-办公-细胞单元

C-1-Wet Land Park-Cell Unit

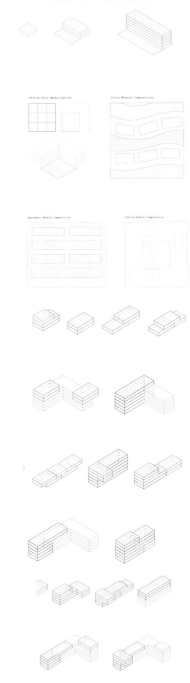

A-4-Villa-Urban Unit
A-4-别墅-城市单元

A-5-Apartment-Urban Unit
A-5-公寓-城市单元

B-4-Villa-Subdivision Unit
B-4-别墅-次级单元

B-5-Apartment-Subdivision Unit
B-5-公寓-次级单元

C-4-Villa-Cell Unit
C-4-别墅-细胞单元

C-5-Apartment-Cell Unit
C-5-公寓-细胞单元

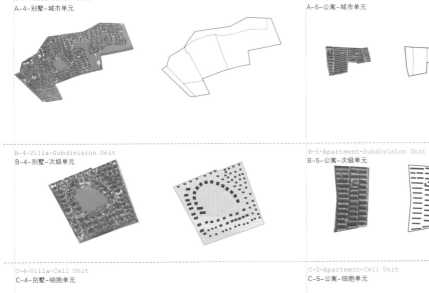

MASTER PLAN
总平面图

CONCEPTUAL COLLAGE
概念示意图

SCHEMATIC RENDERING 1
方案透视图1

SCHEMATIC RENDERING 2
方案透视图2

Isometric Layers

Villa

Office

Apartment

Village Housing

Existing Green

Added Green

Unit Green

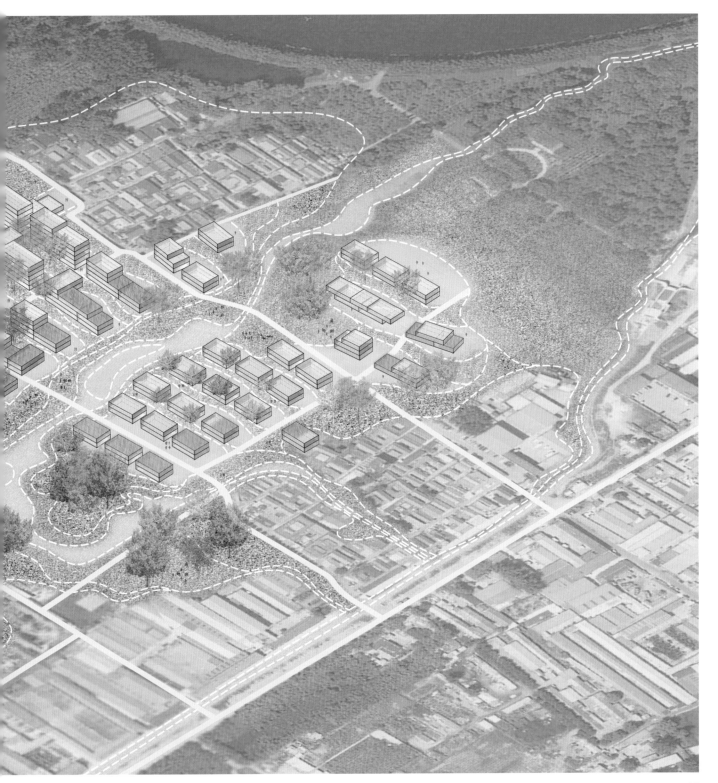

SOIL AND CIRRUS

A model for hybridized space for 21 century peri urban Beijing

Benjamin Scheerbarth

土壤与卷云

21世纪北京城郊混合空间模型

Nanshahe lies at a crossroads. An absence of intervention will translate into insensitive urbanization taking hold of the site. This project poses an alternative model for peri-urban sites, preserving villages through the sharing of resources. Not unlike jazz music, each village is able to play a solo because of a shared framework, freedom because of dependence. This shared framework is in essence a land-use framework.

Specifically, land use is utilized not only as a set of programmatic categories but also as an instrument for guiding form. Traditional land-use categories are questioned and replaced with three spaces of being: the space of the household, the space of cultivation and production, and the space of contemplation and celebration. To counteract the monocultural land use blocks industrial mechanization has inscribed into the land, and acknowledging a new relationship between immaterial production and physical space, the project sets out to productively merge these spaces by juxtaposing them on a micro-grain scale. This overlay results in five categories, or non-categories: soil and cirrus 1 and 2, the ultimate generic, the extended classroom, and mind and soul.

The eponymous category soil and cirrus 1 is the catalyst of the development. It posits a wetland as a site of production for creative and immaterial labor, for Haidian's large population of students and knowledge workers as well as artists, who have traditionally been drawn to the urban edge. Soil and cirrus 2 marries the same category of "light office" with existing agricultural facilities. Adapting to vernacular structures, immaterial labor takes advantage of the agricultural aesthetic. In a way, these two categories are the greenfield equivalent of post-industrial creative appropriation.

南沙河区域正处在一个十字路口。若不主动干预，该区域将会被动地成为城市的一部分。本提案提出一个新的城郊发展模型——通过资源共享来保护现有村庄。跟爵士乐有些相像的是，它们有一个共享的框架存在，每个村庄既能发展自己的特色，又互相联系紧密。这个共享的框架就是用地类型的框架。

具体言之，用地类型不仅仅是程式化的分类，更应该是引导发展形式的工具。传统的用地分类正受到质疑，我们的提案用三种空间取代之：居住空间、生产空间和精神娱乐空间。为了抵制工业机械化时代导致的单一土地利用结构，突出一种物理空间与非物质生产之间的新关系，本提案通过将这些空间与用地类型进行并置而成为五种不同的类型：土壤和卷云1、2，广泛通用，延伸教室以及思想与灵魂。

与本文标题同名的类型-土壤和卷云1将是发展的催化剂，它将湿地视为产生创意和非物质性劳动成果的场所，对象包括海淀区大量的学生、知识工作者以及常常聚集在城市周边的艺术工作者。土壤和卷云2将轻型办公与农业设施结合起来。通过适应本土的环境，非物质性的劳动者能够得益于农业景观美学。在某种程度上，这两个类型相当于后工业时代城市的创意基地。

1900 BUILT-UP AREA
1900年已建区域

1978 WORK UNITS
1978年单位

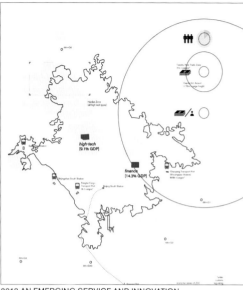

2013 AN EMERGING SERVICE AND INNOVATION ECONOMY IN THE URBAN MOMENT
2013 服务业与创新产业的合并创造了新的城市面貌

Office [Guo Mao CBD]
办公（国贸商务中心区）

Agricultural [Ba Xian Zhuang]
农业（八仙庄）

Institutional [Wudaokou]
工业（五道口）

Residential [Guo Zhuang Zi]
居住（郭庄子）

Industrial [Shou Gang]
工业（首钢）

Postindustrial re-use [798 area]
后工业利用（798地区）

FUNCTIONAL CITY
功能分区

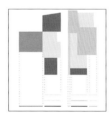

CLOSE-GRAINED DIVERSITY
封闭的分级多样性

MERGING OF LANDUSE IN THE DIGITAL AGE?
在数码时代–合并城市用地性质？

HYPOTHETICAL CHAIN OF WETLANDS ALONG THE NANSHA RIVER
对南沙河沿岸湿地的设想

Introduction of "soil and cirrus" wetland
引入"土地卷云"湿地

Village preservation through shared resources
通过共享资源保护村庄

Civic core extending into three village hearts
城市中心扩展到三个村庄核心

Productive village hinterlands
具有生产效益的村庄

Diffusing the classroom onto village edges
模糊村庄的界限

Allowing new circulations and connections
引入新的流线和连接

 the household
- single-family
- multi-family
- highrise

 cultivation and production
- retail and commercial
- office
- light office
- agricultural facility
- industrial

   contemplation and celebration
- urban green
- wetland
- water
- institutional
- public amenity

 soil and cirrus 1
- wetland
- light office

 soil and cirrus 2
- agricultural facility
- light office

 the ultimate generic
- single-family
- light office
- retail/commercial

 the extended classroom
- wetland
- institutional
- multi-family

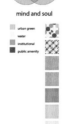 mind and soul
- urban green
- water
- institutional
- public amenity

 soil and cirrus 1
 soil and cirrus 2
the ultimate generic
the extended classroom
mind and soul

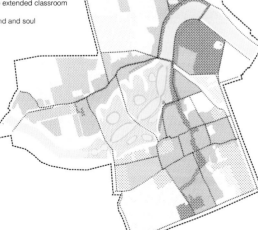

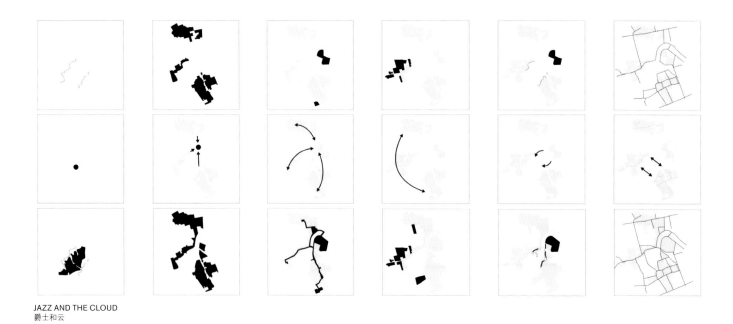

JAZZ AND THE CLOUD
爵士和云

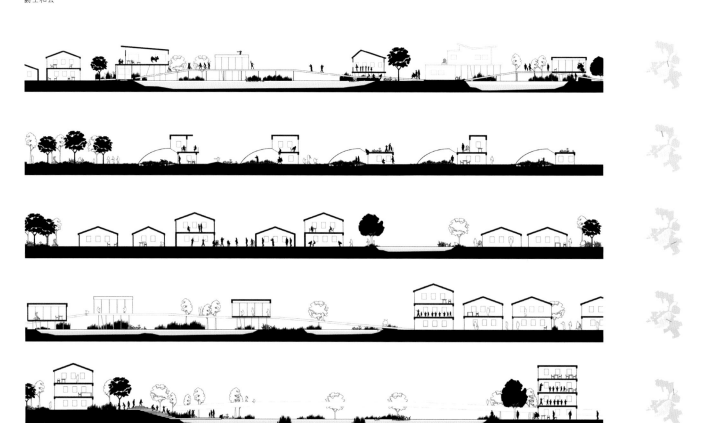

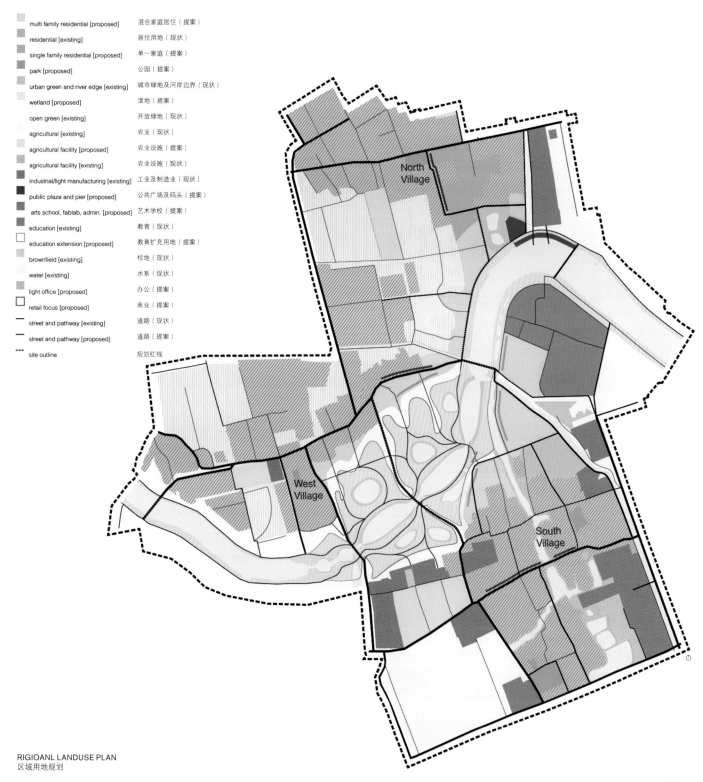

multi family residential [proposed]	混合家庭居住（提案）
residential [existing]	居住用地（现状）
single family residential [proposed]	单一家庭（提案）
park [proposed]	公园（提案）
urban green and river edge [existing]	城市绿地及河岸边界（现状）
wetland [proposed]	湿地（提案）
open green [existing]	开放绿地（现状）
agricultural [existing]	农业（现状）
agricultural facility [proposed]	农业设施（提案）
agricultural facility [existing]	农业设施（现状）
industrial/light manufacturing [existing]	工业及制造业（现状）
public plaza and pier [proposed]	公共广场及码头（提案）
arts school, fablab, admin. [proposed]	艺术学校（提案）
education [existing]	教育（现状）
education extension [proposed]	教育扩充用地（提案）
brownfield [existing]	棕地（现状）
water [existing]	水系（现状）
light office [proposed]	办公（提案）
retail focus [proposed]	商业（提案）
street and pathway [existing]	道路（现状）
street and pathway [proposed]	道路（提案）
site outline	规划红线

North Village

West Village

South Village

RIGIOANL LANDUSE PLAN
区域用地规划

WATERSCAPE
滨水空间

A POPULAR HANG OUT, ESPECIALLY AT SUNSET. ACROSS THE RIVER ONE VIEWS THE SCHOOLS AND UPSTREAM THE WETLAND.
邻水开放空间，日落欢聚场所，河对岸为学校及湿地。

AFTERWORD

Stephen Ervin

后记

In the exercise recorded here, a dozen Harvard graduate students, mixed in international background and disciplinary specialty, were asked to imagine alternative futures in China, for the region of the Nansha river, North West of Beijing, in the Haidian district. In their initial visit to the study area, they found an abused and marginally functional river surrounded by a patchwork of agricultural, industrial, residential, and abandoned lands, at the rapidly expanding edge of the central city's dense urban development. The well-worn villages and recently built high-rise towers of the area are home to tens of thousands——depending on who is counted, and when, and how——of residents, some farming ancestral lands, others recently arrived in search of income and opportunity in modern China. The river, the landscape, the villages and their people are not without their beauty, strength, and integrity. But some of these are compromised, and all are challenged by the modern peri-urban condition in which a clash of cultures, technologies, traditions, expectations, and aspirations are visible at every turn. Despoiled waters, dysfunctional civic infrastructures, extreme income disparities, disrupted ecosystems, polluted air and land, and considerable dynamic flux from season to season and year to year, in both natural and man-made systems, are evident.

The challenges facing this landscape and these people were mirrored in the challenges confronted by these 12 Harvard students. Working in a compressed timeframe, exploring an unfamiliar set of people – land– water interactions, with an alien language, unfamiliar (albeit delicious) food, and often confounding cultural customs, laws, and conventions, they were asked to conceive of a "new commune" embedded in a rejuvenated hydrological, ecological, and socio-economic matrix. "Re-weaving fluxes" was one mandate for the design

　　在本次的课程设计中，来自不同国家和专业学科的12位哈佛大学设计学院学生，对位于北京西北面的南沙河片区进行了一次未来新型城市的构想。他们初次参观该区域的时候看到，南沙河周边已经被快速、高密度发展的城市所包围。河道周围满布农田、工业、居住区和废弃的用地，并且河道在生产和生活中被过度利用，功能衰退。河道周边的老旧村落以及新建的高层建筑里居住着数万人（取决于统计的对象，时间以及方法），包括世代在此耕作的农民以及一些刚刚进城寻找工作机会的新移民。南沙河，当地景观，村落和当地的居民确有他们的美感、力量和完整性，但是或多或少都已经受到了破坏，更是受到了充斥每个角落的文化、科技、传统、期望和抱负激烈碰撞的城郊环境挑战。被掠夺的水资源、功能失常的市政基础设施、巨大的贫富差距、被破坏的生态系统、受污染的水体和土壤，以及自然和人工系统里日日夜夜，年复一年的动态流，这些都有目共睹。

　　这12位哈佛学生的挑战并不亚于当地景观和居民面对的挑战。在有限的时间内，他们需要立即投入到探索自己并不熟悉的人—土地—水体之间的相互关系的任务中。在语言不通，食物不适应（虽然美味），文化习俗、法律和传统使人手足无措的情况下，他们需要构想出一个能恢复水体循环、生态系统功能以及顺应经济社会发展的新社区。"重塑流"是本次设计项目的必需元素，目的在于寻找和修复从前土地、水体和人之间的联系，同时针对当前的现实提出富有想象力的策略。数周以后，他们回到书桌

program, meant to emphasize finding and repairing broken historic connections between land, water, and people, as well as bringing imaginative new approaches reflecting new realities. Then, in a dozen or so weeks, back at their desks with their computers, maps and photographs, students were required to create a compelling story about their imagined alternative future and its impact upon the people, the land, and the river, at both the local and the larger regional scale, taking into account the overlapping spheres of influence of Beijing's inexorable expansion.

In this challenging task the students were forced to confront both universal themes, and local micro-variation. Their strategies had to make sense for individual residents——farmers, entrepreneurs, creative workers, restaurant workers, tourists, temporary residents, and others——as well as at a more abstract social demographic level. The expectation was that their solutions would be both carefully tailored to the unique circumstances of the study area, and also provide a model applicable along the entire length of the Nansha river, or, as many students decided, as a new component of Beijing's ambitious, and only partly successful, encircling greenbelt strategy.

Working alone and in teams of two, using maps, photographs, sketches, fieldnotes, and satellite images, they catalogued, analyzed, synthesized, and integrated a wide range of conditions and multiple competing criteria. Sometimes a designer thinking spatially was working daily with a planner thinking in terms of policies and social behavior. In this they were practicing and experiencing the reality of modern landscape architecture and planning: global in its scope, grounded in the land and natural fluxes, and inextricably linked to the lives of the people of the region.

上，利用电脑、地图和图片来描绘他们构想的南沙河未来愿景，并阐释该设计如何影响当地的人、土地和河流。考虑到北京不可抵挡的扩张现状，针对本地提出的方案实际上具有更大区域尺度上的借鉴意义。

在这个富有挑战性的任务中，学生们需要同时面对普遍的全球性城市化挑战和多样的本地环境。他们提出的策略应当既对当地的个体—农民、企业家、创意产业工作者、餐馆员工、旅客、暂住人口和其他群体产生积极的影响，也应该在抽象的社会人群层面上具有借鉴意义。我们希望他们提供的解决办法既能够细致地对应研究区域的特殊环境，又可以作为整个南沙河两岸发展的示范模型，或者像很多学生提出的，能够补充成为目前不够成功的北京环形绿带策略的一部分。

学生们两人一组，各自分工，利用地图、图片、草图、外业记录、卫星图等材料，分类、分析、总结和综合一系列的环境状况和多个指标。有时，负责空间分析的学生与负责政策与社会行为分析的学生一起合作，这种方式能够让他们实践并体会真实的景观建筑和设计的工作方式：视野全球化，以土地和自然流为基础，并与当地人们的生活紧密地联系在一起。

六个小组分别负责六个不同的主题，他们需要从不同的主题角度进行观察并提出设计方案，包括水体、聚落模式、农业实践、基础设施建设、交通、能源等。这些迥异的主题使得他们的设计方案在设计手段、逻辑和表达上都

Six different teams of two looked at the landscape, each through a different thematic lens, and developed proposals that variously addressed hydrological issues, settlement patterns, agricultural practices, issues of infrastructure, transportation, and energy, and so on. These thematic views gave rise to design proposals that differed dramatically in their means, mechanisms, and representations, but all with often shared visions and overlapping ends. This is the power of design: that similar approaches by similar planners and designers can give rise to a kaleidoscopic variety of possibilities and approaches. The success of this enterprise is not best measured by the reality, or immediate feasibility, of any of these proposals——although some are more immediately realizable than others——rather the success is exactly in the diversity, creativity, and the depths of these proposals.

This project is the fifth in a series of planning and design exercises jointly offered by Harvard Graduate School of Design and Peking University, under the guidance of Professor Kongjian Yu, undertaken by graduate students in and around Beijing, each grappling with some, but never all, of the many complex issues inherent in landscape architecture and planning: sustainable urban and agricultural development, intelligent energy, waste, and transportation systems, beautiful and functional places for people to live, work, and play, along with a myriad of other considerations and criteria, vexing dilemmas and seemingly insoluble problems. We can only hope that in the coming decades these students will go on in their professional lives to develop their skills and insights, to address such pressing problems not only in China, but throughout the developed and developing world, wherever patterns for safe and sustainable settlement and civilization are sought.

产生巨大的差异，但是他们常常会形成相似的愿景。这便是设计的奇妙：相似的规划设计师以相似的方法设计的作品却能产生万花筒般多样的可能性。虽然一些设计方案的确更容易实现，但是本次课程设计的成功与否，最好的评价标准并不在于现实性或立即可实现性，而在于此方案在多样性、创造性和深度上的表现水平。

本课程设计是哈佛大学设计学院和北京大学联合设计实践的第五次合作，由俞孔坚教授指导研究生在北京完成。每位学生选取一些但不是所有的景观规划领域议题进行深入研究。这些议题包括：可持续城市与农业发展，智能能源、废弃物处理，交通系统，良好的居住、工作和娱乐空间，以及一系列棘手的问题和看似难以调和的矛盾。我们希望在未来，学生能够在专业实践中继续发展他们的专业技能和洞察力，不仅为解决中国目前的急迫问题，也为其他发达国家和发展中国家对安全、可持续社会的追求作出贡献。